I0213422

PRINCIPLES OF WHOLENESS
ENDORSEMENTS

"*Principles of Wholeness* is sure to be on your reference shelf for easy access. Key issues are dealt with and keen wisdom is offered. It is full of illustrations that send the message home along with questions sure to stretch you and lead to easy discussion."

Dean Arp, President of Arp Engineering

"If you have ever wondered what it would be like to have a life coach, pick up and read *Principles of Wholeness* by Dr. Steven Jirgal. It is clear, relevant, and practical, addressing issues necessary for living a satisfying, fruitful life. My suggestion: read the conclusion again and again after you read each chapter. It does a terrific job of teaching you how to apply truth to daily life. I found the conclusion to be as helpful as anything I have ever read on how to apply the truth you learn to how you live. You would be well-served by reading the latest from the pen of Dr. Jirgal."

Dr. Charles Kelley, President of New Orleans Baptist Theological Seminary.

"If you've struggled with inadequacy, brokenness, or being haunted by past mistakes (and who among us hasn't?), then *Principles of Wholeness* is a must read. I like how Steve weaves in examples from other people to let us know that we are not alone in what we face. The truth of what he shares is a like a GPS to guide us to a place of godly wholeness, having grown out of our own imperfect weakness to enjoy a life where we are free to live and serve the way in which we were meant."

Joe Paulo, Director of Broadcasting-WRCM, 91.9

"Insightful, Timely, Captivating. Just a few words to describe *Principles of Wholeness*. This is a much needed book sure to help those of us who face life's challenges on a daily basis."

Colin Pinkey, Executive Director of the Harvest Center and NBA Chaplain for the Hornets.

"Sometimes you need some 'Principles' that you can 'Hang Your Hat On' so that you can do some 'Good Thinking'! Well, Steve Jirgal has done just that for you and me. Get a cup of dark roast coffee -- or latte' and 'Hang some truths' on your heart."

Dr. Dennis Swanberg, America's Minister of Encouragement

"All of us limp through life at one time or another and *Principles of Wholeness* is an excellent resource for those times. It weaves together timeless directives and illustrations that are easily applied and adapted to the ever-changing challenges we face."

Perry Tuttle, Clemson University and NFL Receiver.

"A book loaded with hope! *Principles of Wholeness* is a mandatory read for all of us who at some point need a boost! By applying these principles and making the necessary adjustments life can take on new meaning and hope can be reborn."

Robert Walker, Publisher of *Sports Spectrum* Magazine

DR. STEVEN A. JIRGAL

PRINCIPLES OF WHOLENESS

Becoming Whole In A Fractured World

Visit our website:
www.thecoremediagroup.com

Published by The Core Media Group, Inc., P.O. Box 2037, Indian Trail, NC 28079.

Printed in the United States of America.

This book is dedicated to Stephen and Kathryn Crotts. You are truly examples of faithfulness, commitment, love, balance, and friendship. Thank you for speaking life into us on so many levels. God bless you!

In Him,

Steve and Pam

CONTENTS

FOREWORD

Life is full of possibilities and opportunities. Life also carries with it basic principles. These are not guarantees. They are simply principles that when adhered to have a tendency to change the outcome of your life for the better.

It is an honor to introduce to you Dr. Steve Jirgal. As a pastor, father & husband Steve has the heart to speak to you. However as a former athlete, a mentor to many athletes, & a person whose career has spanned the movie industry to the pulpit, Steve has the expertise to interpret the times & culture you live in & the expertise to share a correct response to those challenges. I strongly recommend that if your desire is to thrive as a child of God, to read & heed this book. I prayerfully hope that God will reveal Himself to you as you search these pages and apply these principles.

Dr. Joe B. Brown
Former Sr. Pastor-Hickory Grove Baptist Church

PREFACE

It was a beautiful spring afternoon in the mountains of North Carolina. I was working alone (bad idea) on a cabin my wife and I had always dreamed of building. The air was crisp and fresh and my body was full of energy. I was making great progress and everything was coming together. There was a joy in my heart and a song on my lips. That all changed in an instant. While standing on some scaffolding, I lifted a wall section and placed it on the platform in front of me. But before I could secure it, it topped away from vertical and fell outside. The weight of the wall leveraged me off the scaffolding backwards and I was catapulted out of the building flying 12 feet out and 18 feet down onto the concrete pavement below.

I was stunned. I felt the blood pooling around my head. I had great pain in my back and chest and struggled to my feet grateful to be alive. I walked around the outside of the house and entered through the front door planning on laying down for a short time in order to stop the bleeding from my head. One deep breath told me I was in real trouble. Cell phone reception was poor and I had doubts as to whether anyone could find me, so I determined to drive the 16 miles to the hospital.

Hours later it was revealed that I had broken 3 bones in my back, suffered a large open wound in my head, broken a rib, and damaged a kidney. Physically, I was a broken mess.

Years before, I was entering into a new time in ministry with a para-church organization. I had lots of ideas and plenty of resources. Due to the birth of our first son, my wife had resigned her job. We signed a contract on another home and with a contract in hand on our old house moved to Charlotte. Things would be tight, but we would be okay.

Just a few months into the new position a new fiscal year rolled in. Due to a state-wide decision in the ministry, the money we had raised was used elsewhere. Overnight we went from *full go* status to *furlough* status. That meant I would not be paid until a certain financial level was reached. We went from two incomes to none, had two car payments, hospital bills stacking up, and due to the contract falling through on the sale of our house, now had two mortgages to pay. We went through our small savings in short order and in the turn of the calendar page—we were financially broke.

I remember so vividly the night I got the word that my mother was losing her battle with cancer. It was too late to catch a flight home so I spent the night alternating between dozing and prayer not knowing if I would ever see my mother alive again.

The next morning I was raced to the hospital where I found my mother alive but unresponsive. We each took our turn by her bedside and had the opportunity to convey our love to her. I talked to her not being certain that she understood me. I told her what a good mother she was and that I loved her and was so thankful for her. My mother hung on for several hours and then as I watched her, her breathing stopped and she left this world. My heart ached.

This was a woman who was full of fun and laughter. She always had a project or task she was working on. She gave parties and led the athletic booster club. She taught us crafts and stories and was always there to talk to. She was my mother and now she was gone. Until that moment I didn't really understand how much I needed her. I was emotionally crushed.

Brokenness comes to us all—physically, financially, emotionally, socially, spiritually, all the pieces of your life can be bruised, battered, and broken. You may not see it coming, but it comes. The real question is what will you do once injury enters your life? The pieces will be handed back to you but then it is up to you to fit the pieces together and make your life work again. I know you can do it. And as you turn the following pages, you'll learn how.

INTRODUCTION

The 1997 movie *As Good as it Gets* portrays the life of Melvin Udall, played by Jack Nicholson a highly successful novelist beset with quirks and disorders. In the movie Udall seems to have what so many desire. He's a best-selling author who lives in New York City and has reached the pinnacle of success in the publishing world. However, his behavior and attitude leave him alone and afraid as he alienates everyone with whom he comes in contact.

To describe the career of Heath Ledger as meteoric does not do it justice. He had major roles in nineteen movies including *The Patriot, A Knight's Tale,* and *The Dark Knight.* He won numerous awards from "Best Actor" to "Best Supporting Actor" and seemed to have the world on a string. He was rich, talented, famous, and successful, but on January 22, 2008, he was found dead of a prescription drug overdose.

Junior Seau was a 6'3" 250 pound bone-crushing NFL linebacker. He played for the Chargers, Dolphins, and Patriots. He was an "All-Pro" ten times and selected to the Pro Bowl twelve times and is a member of the NFL's "All Decade" team for the 1990's. He was rich, famous, and respected. But on May 2, 2012, at the age of 43, that all ended when he pressed a gun against his chest and pulled the trigger.

The examples are numerous. I could write of Ernest Hemingway, Kurt Cobain, Freddie Prinze, or Vincent van Gogh. The names and occupations range from Cleopatra to Virginia Woolf and everyone in between. They had status, privilege, wealth, and success. One other thing they each had in common: something was missing. Whether the names are represented in fiction or in real life, these are examples of people whose lives lacked wholeness or completeness. There was a part or several parts that were missing and the recognition of such led to their undoing.

The mental and emotional condition of each of them is summed up well by Albert Einstein, "It is strange to be known so universally and yet be so lonely."

Fame is not enough! Money and possessions are not enough! Achievement is not enough! Those who have had all that knew this. They each came to the same conclusion: something is missing!

Lacking wholeness doesn't encompass having a bad day or suffering a set-back. Life is full of twists and turns and unwelcomed events. Difficult times are sure to come. A lack of wholeness involves a lifestyle of intrinsic voids. It's possessing deep and lasting empty spots at the core of your being. It's found on the soul level. Being whole, however, means possessing the ability to function in various areas of your life sometimes simultaneously in an efficient, consistent, and morally acceptable way. It includes knowing yourself completely and being satisfied with what you know.

A lack of wholeness involves a lifestyle of intrinsic voids. It's possessing deep and lasting empty spots at the core of your being. It's found on the soul level.

You are about to study various principles (not guarantees) that, when applied, will put you on the path to wholeness. For some, this will be a difficult journey filled with heartache and pain as you uncover the source of your internal difficulties. For others, you'll find this to be a great resource for future reference for yourself or one you care about. Regardless of the need, you'll find this work to be enlightening, helpful, and perhaps even life changing. May the Lord bless you as you pursue a life of wholeness.

PRINCIPLE #1
WHOLENESS IS POSSIBLE FOR YOU

"NOT ONLY STRIKE WHILE THE IRON IS HOT, BUT MAKE IT HOT BY STRIKING." -OLIVER CROMWELL

For some, this first principle seems unnecessary to mention. For others, who have been struggling for so long, it's a principle that is all but given up on. Nonetheless, it is where we must start. You must first believe that becoming whole is possible.

In the 1950's Curt Richter from Johns Hopkins Medical School ran an experiment using a number of rats. He placed the rats in a container that was about eight inches wide and held thirty inches of water. As rats are poor swimmers, he timed each of the rats and noted how long it took for each of them to drown. He found that the average rat could swim for about fifteen minutes before giving up and dying. Then he took a number of rats and placed them each in the container. Each of these however, was lifted from the container and allowed to recover. After a short recovery time, they each were placed back in the container. After doing this several times, it was found that they were able to swim in excess of sixty hours. What made the difference? One word—"Hope."

The average person can live for about three to six minutes without oxygen to the brain. You can live for about three days without water and three weeks without food. But you can't take your next step without hope. You've got to have hope! Without hope, life carries no meaning. Without hope, progress can't be made. Without hope, life is not worth living. So to give you as the first principle the possibility of wholeness is to give you hope. To open the door to the very real concept of wholeness is to open the door to something that you may have been missing for a very long time-hope. If you know you can be made whole, you take the next step toward making that a reality.

Having understood that, you must now know that the first place to begin your journey is in your mind. Your mind is the launching pad of your life. It will direct where and how you move forward from this point on. So changes have got to be made in the thinking process. You must first believe that wholeness is possible, and you must next be willing to adjust your thinking and attitude to bring about the changes necessary to foster wholeness.

Your mind is the launching pad of your life. It will direct where and how you move forward from this point on. So changes have got to be made in the thinking process.

Several years ago, I visited the coca cola distribution center in our area. While waiting to pick up some products, I noticed a large bin by the loading dock filled with cans. The cans were full but were badly damaged. I asked about them and was told that the company never allows damaged cans to go on the shelves in stores. If they are slightly damaged, they are put in machines, but if badly damaged, they are sent back to the warehouse and placed in large bins. Of course, I couldn't let the story end there. "Now what?" I asked. I was informed that the cans were each put on a conveyer belt and sliced open. The metal was recycled and the syrup was collected in cylinders and sold to bee keepers. The keepers opened the cylinders in the center of their hives and this increases the productivity of the bees. How creative!

I wonder who came up with that idea. What was going through their head? Regardless of how they got there, it required them to think totally outside the frame of the original use for soda. They had to go in an entirely different direction. You may have to do the same as you seek wholeness.

You have got to understand that life can get better. There are solutions to your problems and answers to your questions. But they all involve two things: changing your mind and changing your habits.

Changing your mind.

For too long you've been hearing a voice in your head shouting at you, *you will never make it. You'll never amount to anything. This is all there is and all there ever will be.* You have got to stop listening to those voices in your head and begin to do the talking. It doesn't matter what life throws at you. What's important is what you do with what life throws at you. What you will find is that life is made up of a series of six -month increments. In those six months, you will find yourself going into or coming out of some type of crisis. It may be your own personal situation or it could be the issues that flow out of a close friend or loved one. How you view that crisis will make all the difference in how you handle it. If you don't really believe you'll be successful, then your chances have just been diminished noticeably.

Proverbs 23:7 says, "For as he thinks within himself, so he is." Abraham Lincoln penned it this way, "A man is what he thinks about all day long." Isn't it time you changed your thinking? But it's not enough to decide you're going to change your thinking. You have to replace the wrong thoughts with the right ones.

Recently, one of the escort vehicles assigned as part of the President's entourage had to be towed away. The problem? The driver pulled into a gas station and filled up the tank with diesel fuel when it ran on gasoline. Was it wrong to fill it up? Certainly not! But the engine was meant to run on regular gas, not diesel. It was topped off with the wrong fuel. Too often that's what happens in our thinking. We open ourselves up to new thoughts, but they're the wrong ones.

If you plan on experiencing wholeness, you've got to determine to change your mind. The reason so many people can't start a new chapter in their lives is because they're too busy re-reading an old one.

Often, when you talk to people, you can get a clear picture of where their thinking is. Some are stuck in the past. All they think about and subsequently talk about is what happened to them, how it used to be, or how life has not been fair. If that is a description of your mentality, I have some news for you! In fact, I have great news for you! This news is so good that I have to shout it to you: YOUR PAST IS NOT YOUR FUTURE!

I want to invite you to think about your car. Have you noticed that your windshield is vastly larger than your rear-view mirror? That being the case, doesn't it make sense to spend more time focusing on the road ahead instead of the road behind? That is the way you should be looking at your life. This is not to call you to live in denial of the things in your past. It's simply an encouragement to spend most of your time thinking about where you're going instead of where you've been. If you plan on experiencing wholeness, you've got to determine to change your mind. The reason so many people can't start a new chapter in their lives is because they're too busy re-reading an old one.

Changing your habits.

There is an old adage that says, "If you always do what you've always done, you'll always be where you always were." If you want your life to change, you've got to change some of the habits you've developed that have become barriers to change.

When I counsel couples struggling in their marriage, invariably I'll ask them, "Do you want your marriage to work?" Though it sounds like a strange question, it's no secret that if both of them are not interested in the marriage working, they are destined to fail. The next question involves a commitment level. "Are you willing to make the changes necessary to make your marriage work?" Again, both must answer in the affirmative. It's obvious that wanting something to go well is much easier than working to have it go well. It's the difference between wanting to play the piano and being willing to take lessons and practice to make it happen.

For change to take place, a change in the will and an infusion of energy are required. It often involves experiencing pain.

When Jesus was at the pool of Bethesda, He came upon a man who had been crippled for 38 years. He looked at the man and asked a question that must have seemed foolish to all those around. "Do you want to get well?" What a question! Of course the man wanted to be healed. Who wouldn't? But by digging a bit deeper we'll be able to see that the question was not so foolish. You see, getting better meant no more begging, no more free handouts. It meant moving out of his circle of friends he'd grown comfortable with. It meant no more pity and no more excuses. It called for accountability, responsibility, a job. Maybe that question was more called for than we first thought.

But change is never automatic and not always welcome. For change to take place, a change in the will and an infusion of energy are required. It often involves experiencing pain. In fact, change will not happen in a person's life until the pain of staying the same is greater than the pain of change.

One sunny afternoon a salesman stopped by a country store seeking directions. There were a few elderly men in overalls sitting on the front porch. They were glad to give him directions, but the salesman noticed something very strange. The entire time he was talking to the gentlemen, a large dog was lounging on the porch. The dog was lying on its side and whimpering and whining the entire time. After getting directions he felt compelled to ask, "What's wrong with that old dog? He's been crying the whole time I've been talking to you." One of the old men explained, "Well that old boy happens to be lying on a nail that sticking up from the porch." "Well, why doesn't he move?" the man asked. "Well, I guess he doesn't hurt enough," the old man explained.

As you make a close evaluation of your life, ask yourself this question: Do I hurt enough to make the changes in my behavior and my thinking which are necessary in order for me to experience wholeness?

You'll find that changes you have to make whether physical, spiritual, mental, or in any other domain may include results that were not caused by you. Car accidents, physical, mental, or sexual abuse, loss of a loved one, disease, the divorce of parents, or other factors may be beyond your control. Though these problems were not caused by you and thereby not your fault or responsibility, your reaction to them is. You will indeed have to choose how you are going to play the hand you've been dealt. You have to choose to make the changes in your mind if you are ever going to see changes in your life. If wholeness is going to come your way, you've got to embrace the adjustments that need to be made and you need to do that immediately.

Make no mistake about it. The devil does not want you to experience wholeness. He wants you to live a defeated life blaming God for everything that goes wrong. You must resist him. One of the greatest temptations the devil and his minions use against the believer is delay. If he can get you off the mark and cause you to develop a "not today" attitude regarding positive changes in your life, he may be able to cause you to put it off indefinitely.

In order for you to embrace the idea of becoming whole, you have to admit that it's possible. That means you must embrace the entire concept of wholeness. You must say to yourself (even out loud), "I can become whole!"

Remember, a set-back is a set-up for a comeback.

When you have arrived at that conclusion, your next area of focus must be on the action steps necessary to establish the momentum needed to take that concept and make it a reality. Here is what comes next:

1-Set Goals. Without goals you will tend to wander aimlessly. You've got to have a measuring stick in order to chart your progress.

2-Be accountable. You need to share your quest for wholeness with someone you can trust. It must be someone close enough to feel comfortable in asking you some very invasive questions regarding your progress and effort.

3-Make the right choices. So much of the progress we make in our lives hinges on making right or wrong choices. Quite often we know the correct choice to make but because of the difficulty of the task we avoid going in the right direction. The fact is, the choices you make today determine the opportunities you have tomorrow.

4-Seek good counsel. You become what you surround yourself with. The group of people you move in and around will either take you up or take you down. You must be honest in the evaluation of your peers. They are either helping you or hindering you from becoming whole. Seek out someone whom you hold in high regard due to wisdom and experience. Ask this person for help on your journey.

5-Be determined. "I'm going to get better." Wholeness is not something that will come to you automatically. You are going to have to work at it and at times it may get very difficult. You must push through the barriers that get in the way of your getting what you really want-wholeness. You must be consistent in this!

6-Rely on God. God will always be there for you. He is just waiting for you to call on Him for help. He will bring you the answers you need at the moment you need them. Generally, you will see God intervening in your life in at least one of four ways: Through people, His word, His Holy Spirit in you, or special circumstances He arranges for your life. Try to remain sensitive to the ways God is waiting to assist you.

7-Expect set-backs. Because wholeness is not easily obtained, you will experience times when things aren't going so well and you may not be making any noticeable progress. Remember, a set-back is a set-up for a come-back. Push through those difficult times understanding that everyone experiences times and seasons where progress is slow and even non-existent.

SHARING PIECES:

What drains you of your hope?

Share about a time when you felt the most hopeful. What led to that?

What do you most often find your thoughts centering on?

What will it take for you to redirect your thinking?

From whom do you most often seek counsel? Why?

PRINCIPLE #2
YOU CAN TRUST GOD

"I BELIEVE IN THE SUN EVEN WHEN IT IS NOT SHINING. I BELIEVE IN LOVE EVEN WHEN I FEEL IT NOT. I BELIEVE IN GOD EVEN WHEN HE IS SILENT." -(WRITTEN ON A WALL IN A CONCENTRATION CAMP.)

The world yearns for wholeness. People want to be comfortable with themselves and accepted by those around them. But life gets in the way and so often breaks us and shatters us into pieces and brings to light the idea that in and of ourselves we are damaged goods. In 1967, Thomas A. Harris published a book titled *I'm O.K., You're O.K.* It was embraced far and wide not because it was true but because we so desperately wanted it to be true. However, when the smoke cleared, we found, much to our dismay and disappointment, that we're simply not O.K. As we travel along in life, we pick up scars, warts, and broken dreams. Life is not perfect and neither are we.

You must find something to trust in. You must find something that is reliable, steadfast, and unmovable. If you lean on whatever the world itself presents, you will be greatly disappointed.

So we must go outside of ourselves and find a way to "fix" that which is broken in us. But where do we go to mend the broken pieces? The world's recipe for wholeness includes things like, "Take this... Eat this... Drink this. Buy this...Experience this..." But after following the world's manual for wholeness, we find that some of the parts are still missing. Now what?

One thing is certain. You must find something to trust in. You must find something that is reliable, steadfast, and unmovable. If you lean on whatever the world itself presents, you will be greatly disappointed. Fashions, tastes, gimmicks, and fads all change, and if you rely on them to make you whole, you will find yourself changing your pursuits as often as you change your car's oil.

The story is told of a Navy destroyer heading for home. The captain was informed that there was a vessel spotted off the bow and coming straight at them. The captain instructed his signal flasher to flash the message, "Adjust your course 20 degrees west." In moments the signal came back and said, "Negative. Please adjust your course 20 degrees east." The captain was incensed. He ordered another message to be sent. "This is Captain Olsen of the U.S. Navy. Adjust your course 20 degrees west." The word was returned, "This is John Donnelly. Adjust your course 20 degrees east." The captain was outraged. The next message was very abrupt. "Adjust your course 20 degrees west immediately! I am a Navy destroyer." The next message was equally abrupt. "Adjust your course 20 degrees east immediately! I am a lighthouse!"

There are certain things that you would do best not to ask to move. They are steady and remain in place. A lighthouse is one of them. God is another. Psalm 18:2 tells us, "The Lord is my rock and my fortress and my deliverer, my God my rock, in whom I take refuge; my shield and the horn of my salvation, my stronghold." In short, He is unmovable, indestructible, and totally dependable. You can trust Him.

Please keep in mind that your ability to trust in God (or anyone else) comes incrementally. It comes in stages. As you trust God and He proves Himself trustworthy and He always does, you develop the ability to trust Him more.

In Matthew 14:22-33, we find the story of Jesus walking on the water. The disciples are in a boat without Jesus. The wind and waves are giving them trouble. Jesus comes walking on top of the water. He is far enough away from them that they can't readily recognize Him but they can make out a figure of a man on top of the waves. They assume that it is a ghost and are wrapped in fear. Jesus speaks to them and tells them not to be afraid. He is far enough away from them that they still don't recognize Him. Peter calls out, "Lord, if it is you, command me to come to you on the water." The Lord speaks one word to Peter, "Come." That's all it took for this man who was so well acquainted with these waters to get out of the boat and to walk on the water (every fisherman's dream). Bear in mind the sea was not calm. This was not a glass surface Peter was asked to step out on. The wind was still blowing. I don't believe for a moment, that Peter jumped out of the boat. I think rather that he slid one foot out of the boat and felt the surface of the water and noticed that it was solid. Then he lifted the other leg over the edge of the boat and, while still holding onto the boat, stood on the water. Then turning from the boat and letting go, he began his walk toward Jesus. This magnificent experience of Peter was not an all-out abandonment of what he knew to be true: People don't walk on the water every day. People drown out here. This is not normal. Peter trusted the Lord enough to want to walk on top of the water and be with Him. But the trust came in measures. Once he felt the solid surface, he began to walk.

God says, "Trust Me! Rely on me. Rest in Me!" Proverbs 3: 5-6 directs us, "Trust in the Lord with all your heart and do not lean on your own understanding. In all your ways acknowledge Him, and He will make your paths straight."

Why is it that God can show up in incredible ways in your life and you lean on Him without hesitation, but when some minor trouble comes by way of a person or life's circumstance, you get so rattled?

When I was a young boy in New York, my dad took a bunch of us on a hike in the local mountains. We found ourselves on top of a ridge on the edge of a cliff. I watched as my dad unpacked a coil of rope and laid it out. The plan was for us to tie ourselves (using one of the knots he had taught us) to the rope and lean back as we "repelled" over the edge. The rope was strong. My dad was strong. But I did not automatically lean back and give myself freely to the exercise. I eased my way over the edge and kept one hand on the rope and the other on the cliff. Once comfortable with that, I began to lean back and push away from the wall as my dad controlled the rope. As I trusted, he proved trustworthy and I had a great experience. As you trust God, He proves Himself trustworthy and you grow in faith. But you must trust Him enough to be constantly looking for Him and believe that He can be found even in the places where you think He will not be.

Remember Elijah? He had experienced a great victory over the prophets of Baal at Carmel. He trusted God and God came through with flying colors. Then something happened inside of him that caused him to fear the evil queen Jezebel. Here was a guy, God's man, who just won a major victory over the forces of evil, and we find him running from a girl! How can this be? Somehow Elijah took his eyes off the provider and protector of his life and he began to live life by what he felt, not by whom he trusted.

Elijah hid himself for a period in a place outside of Beersheba. Then he traveled for forty days and came to Horeb, the Mountain of God and lodged in a cave. Elijah wrestled with his feelings. He was afraid, frustrated, confused and felt very alone. These feelings were so real and strong that he wanted to die and asked the Lord to take his life.

Then God made His presence known. But it wasn't the way you or I, or Elijah expected it. A strong wind came. The wind was so strong that it moved boulders, after that, an earthquake, and then a fire. But the Lord was in none of these. Elijah felt the presence of God when a soft, gentle breeze blew against him. At that point he knew he was in the presence of Almighty God. At that point he knew that God was in charge. At that point he knew that he could obey and trust the one who had always been faithful.

What will it take for you to loosen the reins a little more and trust the one that never fails? Why is it that God can show up in incredible ways in your life and you lean on Him without hesitation but when some minor trouble comes by way of a person or life's circumstance you get so rattled?

Jennifer knew about this. She had it all. She walked with the Lord. She was in college and was a scholar athlete. She was voted homecoming queen and was the president of a prominent Christian club. But because her boyfriend got into an argument with a guy who was paying her some attention, her world fell apart. She felt that everything in her life was going wrong. Why is that? It is the same for her as it is for us. We lose our trust in God when we do one of three things: we listen to the musings of the devil and his demons; we pay more attention to what someone says and does; we look around and notice the circumstances (wind and waves) in our lives.

What does trusting God look like?

Trusting God more means trusting yourself less. It means trusting your experience, wisdom, common sense, knowledge, and expertise less.

The early disciples found that out. Several of them were fishermen. These were not men who simply enjoyed a day on the banks of the river casting their hooks out into the current. These were veterans of the trade. They fished for a living. They knew what they were doing. Luke 5: 1-7 tells us the story of the calling of the disciples. They had been busy casting their nets all night and came up empty. When Jesus arrived on the scene, they were washing their nets. They gave it their best shot and had nothing to show for it. It was time to call it a night and go home. Jesus got into one of the boats and was teaching the crowd who had gathered on the shore. After speaking for a while, he told Peter to push away into the deep water and let down his nets. Peter responded from a human perspective. He gave his expert answer, "Master, we worked hard all night and caught nothing, but at your bidding, I will let down the nets." Jesus was not a fisherman. The Bible gives us no reference that He had ever fished in His life. *But He was the one who created fish.* The Bible equally gives us no indication that Peter or the other disciples knew the word of God. Yet he put Proverbs 3:5-6 into play. "Trust in the Lord with all your heart and do not lean on your own understanding. In all your ways acknowledge Him and he will make your paths straight." When they did that, they caught more fish than they ever planned. It was such a great catch of fish that they needed two boats to haul it in. Someone said, "God's choices are exactly what you would do if you had all the answers."

The question that must be addressed is why should I trust God?

God has a history of being trustworthy.

Psalm 61:3 says, "For thou has been a refuge for me, a tower of strength against the enemy."

The Israelites lived the history of God's faithfulness. They saw plagues sent against Egypt. They walked on dry land as God parted the Red Sea. They ate the manna sent from God every day. They drank the water sent from the rock. They felt the dust against their faces as the enormous walls of Jericho fell with a shout. Daniel knew God was trustworthy when he spent an entire night in the den of hungry lions. Joseph experienced God's faithfulness when over a period of years he went from being a shepherd boy to the second highest position in Egypt. From this position he was able to provide for his family and ultimately the entire nation of Israel.

Gideon understood the faithfulness of God when he attacked and defeated 135,000 Mideanites with just 300 men. The disciples saw first-hand how Jesus, the God-man, exemplified trustworthiness when He healed the lame, gave sight to the blind, cured the lepers, and raised the dead.

And if you slow down long enough and think with just a little bit of effort, I'm sure you will find that time after time God has proved Himself capable of holding you up and meeting your needs. He has provided for your every need. He has protected you, rescued you, and comforted you when you needed it most and perhaps when you expected it least.

When you are hurt or tired, you look for a wall you can lean on. As you lean on that wall and it holds fast, you learn to lean on it more often and put more of your bone weary weight on it. God's history time and again proves that He is worthy of trust. You can indeed lean on Him.

God has all the resources you'll ever need.

God is everywhere all at once. Psalm 139:7-12 declares, "Where can I go from Thy Spirit? Or where can I flee from Thy presence? If I ascend to heaven, Thou art there; if I make my bed in Sheol, behold, Thou art there. If I take the wings of the dawn, if I dwell in the remotest part of the sea, even there Thy hand will lead me, and Thy right hand will lay hold of me. If I say, 'surely the darkness will overwhelm me, and the light around me will be night,' even the darkness is not dark to Thee, and the night is as bright as the day. Darkness and light are alike to Thee."

This is called omnipresence. We get the faulty idea that God is above the earth and He is reaching His hands around the entire earth and touching everything. While that is a picture that helps us understand the fact that God is able to affect everything all at once, it doesn't explain fully the meaning of omnipresence. The concept is much more abstract and complex. Literally, omnipresence means that all of God is everywhere at the same time. That is how He can address your problems in your home while at the same time deal with a need someone has in a hut in Zimbabwe.

Isaiah 40:10 says, "Behold the Lord God will come with might, with His arm ruling for Him." He is strong enough to carry you and all that concerns you. Nothing is too big for Him and nothing is too small for Him. In fact, the big things to us are little things to God and the little things to us are big things to God.

God created everything that is created by the word of his mouth. In Latin it is called "Ex Nihilo." That means he made everything out of nothing. It is not like he took something someone else made and added to it. There was nothing there and he spoke it into existence. A God that strong can take care of you and whatever might possibly overwhelm you.

Isaiah 55:8-9 tells us, "For my thoughts are not your thoughts, neither are your ways my ways, declares the Lord. For as the heavens are higher than the earth, so are my ways higher than your ways and my thoughts than your thoughts." In short, this means that we cannot figure God out. It would be wise to stop trying. W Glyn Evans reminds us, "Since I cannot fathom God, I must trust Him. I must trust Him not because He promises me things, but because He is good, holy, fair, and does what is right. In other words, I can trust His word, because I can trust His character."

Elisha understood this. He was a prophet of God during a time when the Arameans were oppressing the Israelites. Elisha continually told the king of Israel the location and plans of the Arameans frustrating the army of Aram. When this was told to the king of Aram he located the prophet of God and sent soldiers and chariots to surround the city of Dothan by night and take Elisha captive. In the morning Elisha's servant went out and saw the entire city surrounded by Aramean soldiers. He panicked and reported it to Elisha. But Elisha wasn't alarmed because he had the power of God on his side, and when you know God is in your corner, you do not get intimidated. He told his servant that they were safe because there were more on their side than on the side of the Arameans. Of course, this sounded insane to the servant. But then Elisha asked for the eyes of his servant to be opened and he saw the entire hillside filled with chariots of fire. A scene like that will do wonders for your faith! When you see that, your confidence soars.

Then Elisha asked the Lord to strike the army with blindness and the enemy was blinded and wandered around helplessly. They stumbled into Dothan and were told by Elisha that the one they are looking for is not there but in Samaria and he led them to Samaria where the army of Israel was waiting. Elisha requested their eyes to be opened and when they were, they found themselves the captives of Israel. God can change a situation in a heartbeat.

God loves you.

From a personal standpoint, this is by far the most important attribute of God. Just because God has a history of taking care of others and just because He is perfectly capable of taking care of you that does not guarantee that He will. This is where His unconditional, everlasting, and overpowering love comes in. You matter to God.

Jeremiah 31:3, promises, "I have loved you with an everlasting love."

In fact, God loves you so much it's beyond your ability to understand. Ephesians 3:17-19 says, "…so that Christ may dwell in your hearts through faith; and that you, being rooted and grounded in love, may be able to comprehend with all the saints what is the breadth and length and height and depth, and to know the love of Christ which surpasses knowledge, that you may be filled up to all the fullness of God."

God loves you so much you can't understand it. He loves you even more than you love yourself. In fact, He loves you so much that He wants to spend all of eternity with you and He's willing to die to make that happen. You can trust God because you can trust His character and His motivation.

With these thoughts in mind, you must understand that you can trust God with your finances, health, relationships, education, occupation, desires, safety, and your very soul. In fact, there are no areas that are out-of-bounds from trusting God.

God is not mad at you. He does not wink at your sin but loves you through it and in spite of it. And the love He carries for you is not a fickle kind of love that is here today and gone tomorrow. It does not depend on your response or what you might bring to the relationship. It is total and complete love that is sacrificial by its very nature.

A young girl and her dad would play a game to pass the time while driving in the car. The man would grab his daughter's hand and say, "I love you this much." Then he would squeeze her hand tightly and hold on until his hand grew weary and he had to let go. Then it was the young girl's turn. She would grab her father's big hand with both of hers. She would grit her teeth and squeeze with all she had. After a period of time she would tire and have to let go. One day she turned to her father in frustration and said, "Daddy, I can't hold you long enough or squeeze you hard enough to let you know how much I love you." And so it is with our heavenly Father. He is moving all of creation to squeeze us and hold us long enough to let us know how much He loves us.

What trusting God does:

There are many benefits to trusting God. Over time, with continual growth, by releasing more of your life into His care, you will find areas of your life that will expand.

Over time, with continual growth, by releasing more of your life into His care; you will find areas of your life that will expand.

A-It will strengthen your relationship with God. As you depend on Him more and more, you will find yourself spending more time in prayer, Bible study, and worship. You will tend to gravitate toward the one who does so much for you. "As the deer pants for the water brooks, so my soul pants for Thee, O God." (Psalm. 42:1).

B-Your hope and faith will increase. As you increase your trust in the Lord, your hope in His promises will grow and your reliance on Him for all your needs will increase. You will become a person of faith. However, at the moment you fully enter into His presence (in heaven), you will no longer have faith. Your faith will all be changed to fact. There is no faith in heaven. All the faith that we have carried will be exchanged and we will at that point walk in fact.

You can choose to trust God or you can continue to rely on yourself to the exclusion of God.

C-You will inspire others to grow in their faith. Those who see your life and the way you walk in faith will be motivated to trust God more with their own lives. You will be an example of what God can do when we release our lives to Him. The greatest compliment you will hear is when someone says, "I want to be like you." When people think of particular aspects of the faith, certain names jump to the forefront of their minds. When it's giving, it might be Mother Teresa. In evangelism perhaps it's Billy Graham. What about faith. Maybe when the subject comes up, your face graces the mind of someone who knows you well.

D-Your love for others will increase. This will draw you to share the good news of the gospel with those with whom you come in contact. You will have a testimony to the goodness of God and you will be anxious to share that with all those who will listen. A friend of mine was very natural in the way he shared his faith. I had often been with him and heard him say to someone, "Do you know what I'm excited about today?" Obviously that drew some bystander's interest and then he would share what it was like to have a relationship with Christ and be guaranteed a place in heaven.

So it all comes down to a choice. You can choose to trust God or you can continue to rely on yourself to the exclusion of God. You will find yourself either trusting God or trusting yourself. The following gauge demonstrates the choice you have. The more you trust yourself, the less you trust God and vice versa. This is true with each situation you find yourself in and throughout your entire life.

__________________________I________________________________

YOURSELF GOD

You have stumbled and failed countless times but God has never failed. He has a perfect record. Not once has anything that He promised failed to come true. Not once has he abandoned the ones He loves so deeply. Not once has He made a mistake or poor decision. Because of all of this, you can trust God!

SHARING PIECES:

On a scale of 1-10 (10 being highest), where would you say your level of trust in God lies?

What is the biggest thing you have trusted God with?

In what area of your life would you say you need to trust God more?

Relate a time when you trusted someone who let you down.

PRINCIPLE #3
YOU CAN BE FORGIVEN

"HE WHO CANNOT FORGIVE BREAKS THE BRIDGE OVER WHICH HE HIMSELF MUST PASS." -GEORGE HERBERT

The guilt that comes from not receiving forgiveness is a heavy burden to bear. In essence, unforgiveness comes from one, and possibly all three places: God, others, oneself.

With God, forgiveness is granted by asking. With others, it comes from their granting it. With ourselves, it comes from believing it.

With God, there are two levels of forgiveness that must be asked for:

A-Judicial forgiveness. This falls under the doctrine of justification. It has to do with a person's request for forgiveness and desire to be made a child of God. It is, once and for all, eternal and irrevocable. It is the forgiveness that grants a person entrance to heaven when one steps out of this life. It is this forgiveness that causes God to see Jesus when He looks at us.

Psalm 103:12 says, "As far as the east is from the west, so far has he removed our transgressions from us." The writer uses the directions east and west rather than north and south to demonstrate that these sins will never catch up with the person. If a person heads north long enough, he eventually will be heading south. But if a person heads east or west, he will continue heading in that direction and never switch over to head in the other direction. All my past, present, and future sins will never erase my established relationship with the Father. It is built on faith. The penalty for my sins has been covered by the cross of Christ. Isaiah 53:6 tells us, "All of us like sheep have gone astray, each of us has turned to his own way;" That part of the verse is a fact of life. I'm a sinner. It is in my nature. I'm not a sinner because I sin. I sin because I'm a sinner. The next part is where God steps into the middle of my sin. The rest of Isaiah 53:6 states, "But the Lord has caused the iniquity of us all to fall on him." Romans 8:38-39 says, "For I am convinced that neither death, nor life, nor angels, nor principalities, nor things present, nor things to come, nor powers, nor height, nor depth, nor any other created thing, will be able to separate us from the love of God, which is in Christ Jesus our Lord." Further, Romans 5:8, tells us, "But God demonstrates His own love toward us, in that while we were yet sinners, Christ died for us."

This judicial forgiveness establishes my personal relationship with the Lord. This is the *"spiritual DNA"* that has been established and cannot be altered. I am His child and no matter what I do or how far I wander from Him I cannot change the fact that I am a part of the family of God. That has been established by my acknowledging and embracing the penalty Jesus paid on the cross. This is the forgiveness I receive because Jesus paid the penalty for the sins of mankind on the cross.

I am not suggesting that God possesses the flaw of forgetfulness. I am saying that when we go before our Father and sincerely confess our sins He forgives them and treats the matter as if it never happened.

B-Paternal Forgiveness. Although I cannot lose my place as a child of God, I can however, disrupt by relationship with God Almighty. I do this by committing sin. My standing as a child of God is set, but my relationship with God can become strained due to disobedience.

As a boy, I understood that my parents loved me. I knew that I was part of the family and that I would always carry the family name. All of us knew that. But, there were times when I *sinned* (and some of them were big ones) against my parents. I was still their kid, but my sin caused our relationship to be disrupted. I can remember many evenings when it was very quiet around the dinner table. Confession and forgiveness broke the awkward silence.

Paternal forgiveness hinges on three things:

1-Repentance. Mark 1:4 tells us, "John the Baptist appeared in the desert proclaiming a baptism of repentance for the forgiveness of sins."

2-Confession. I John 1:9 says, "If we confess our sins, He is faithful and righteous to forgive us our sins and to cleanse us from all unrighteousness." In what has been called "the Lord's Prayer," Jesus instructs us to pray and ask for forgiveness for our debts. (Matthew 6:12a).

3-Forgiveness of Others. Continuing on with "The Lord's Prayer" Jesus said, "As we forgive those who sinned against us." Matthew 6:14-15 tells us, "For if you forgive others for their transgressions, your heavenly Father will also forgive you. But if you do not forgive others, then your Father will not forgive your transgressions." This is an uncomfortable scenario. You may be asking, "Are you saying that paternally, I won't be forgiven if I don't forgive others?" No, not at all! It is Jesus who is saying that. He says that our relationship with him is contingent on our relationship with others and that if we expect things to be right between the heavenly Father and us, we have to make them right between us and other people.

What Paternal Forgiveness looks like:

Micah 7:19 promises, "He will again have compassion on us; He will tread our iniquities under foot. Yes, thou wilt cast all their sins into the depths of the sea." Someone has rightly said, "When God casts our sins into the sea, He posts a sign that says, 'No fishing.'" That means by you or by Him. This is exemplified by the story of a woman who claimed that she could speak to God and He would audibly speak to her. Everyone in the village had heard about her. Wanting to test the woman, a priest made his way to her home. After speaking to her for a while, he brought up the subject and asked her to talk to God about a sin he had committed while attending seminary. She left the room and brought the subject before the Lord and in a short time came back to the priest with this answer, "He said He remembers you confessing it and forgot what it was."

I am not suggesting that God possesses the flaw of forgetfulness.

I am saying that when we go before our Father and sincerely confess our sins He forgives them and treats the matter as if it never happened. Isaiah 38:17 promises, "Thou hast cast all my sins behind thy back."

When God looks at the believer's life, He sees the blood of Jesus Christ received by faith and eternal death is bypassed.

Bear in mind three important features of the paternal forgiveness available to us:

1-Forgiveness is a gift from God. We can't earn it and we don't deserve it. Because of God's bountiful love and grace, we can approach Him in repentance and with confidence and He will forgive us every time. It originates from the top and goes down to us, not the other way around. Someone has said that G.R.A.C.E. stands for "God's Riches At Christ's Expense."

2-Forgiveness is immediate. Forgiveness does not happen over time as we distance ourselves from the offense. It does not seep into our souls like water through dirt. That is how we treat each other, but it is not how the Lord treats His children. The second our heart approaches God confessing and repenting, forgiveness is granted.

3-Forgiveness is complete. No matter how vile the offense, there are no sins that are not covered by the blood of Jesus Christ with the exception of blaspheming (denying) the Holy Spirit (Mark 3:28-29). This is a difficult concept to embrace, but without the indwelling of the Holy Spirit, a person cannot have eternal life and without accepting Christ through the Holy Spirit, forgiveness cannot be granted. When God looks at the believer's life, He sees the blood of Jesus Christ received by faith and eternal death is bypassed. This is likened to the Passover in the book of Exodus where the blood of the lamb was placed on and over the doors of followers of Jehovah and the death angel "passed over" without bringing death to that home.

We must trust Him with our sins and take by faith that forgiveness is complete. The world looks at our offenses and says, "You made your bed, now lie in it." But God looks at our offenses and says, "You are forgiven. Now take up your bed and walk."

While camping in the wilderness, a father and daughter were caught unawares by a raging brush fire. They did their best to escape but found themselves surrounded by flames and trapped. Because he had an understanding of fire and nature, the father stooped down and lit the grass on fire where they were standing. The fire quickly spread from where they were and raced toward the flames around them. The father held his daughter as he stepped over the low flames in the grass. In minutes the fire around them had burned out and they were standing in a field of blackened straw. Still fearful, the daughter clung to the neck of the father and cried. Comforting his daughter, the father said, "We are safe. The flames cannot touch us. We are standing where the fire has already been."

And so it is with our sins. The fire of our offense has been extinguished and burnt out. It can no longer harm us. Horatio G. Spafford understood this doctrine when he penned the words to the well-known hymn, "It is Well with My Soul." "My sin, oh the bliss of this glorious thought. My sin, not in part, but the whole-is nailed to the cross and I bear it no more, praise the Lord! Praise the Lord Oh my soul."

We would do well to understand that God's holiness is never adjusted or compromised. Likewise, our sin is never ignored or dismissed without His grace. As we mature in Him we see ever clearer the majesty of His holiness and the depths of our sin.

A new Christian might view God's holiness at a certain level and his own sinfulness at another level. But as he matures, he moves God's holiness higher and his sinfulness lower.

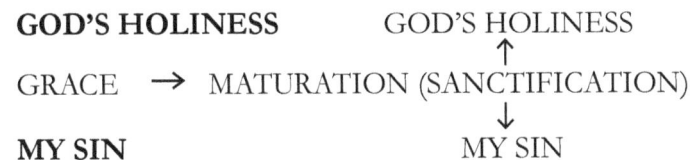

GOD'S HOLINESS GOD'S HOLINESS
↑
GRACE → MATURATION (SANCTIFICATION)
↓
MY SIN MY SIN

God's word tells us, "…but where sin abounded, grace did abound more exceedingly." (Romans 5:20). That means the more we get a handle on God's grace, the more we admit to our sin and understand His holiness.

What unconfessed sin does:

1-It keeps the door open for the continuation of sin. Unless and until you stop your behavior and address the sin in your life, you are apt to continue in that sin. You must call it what it is and not give it a cute and fluffy name as if it were a pet or imaginary friend. Adultery is not an *affair*. Stealing is not *embezzlement*. When a person *shares* some information about someone's sin, that is called nothing other than gossip. *Little white lies* are only big black lies that we have whitewashed to make them more palatable. Stop the sin! Admit what it is and confess it!

2-It weighs you down and inhibits your ministry. Hebrews 12:1 says, "Therefore, since we have so great a cloud of witnesses surrounding us, let us also lay aside every encumbrance and the sin which so easily entangles us, and let us run with endurance the race that is set before us…"

This is shown in the cartoon *Peanuts*. Lucy is seen in the outfield. She has just dropped an easy fly ball. It landed right in her glove and popped out. Charlie asked her why she dropped it and she said, "I was in the right place to catch the ball and then I remembered all the times I dropped the ball. I guess the past got in my eyes." Don't let unconfessed sin get in your eyes and keep you from doing the job you've been called to do.

3-It truncates God's power in you. King David understood that. After his sin with Bathsheba and subsequent cover up attempt by having Uriah killed, he said in Psalm 31:10 and Psalm 32:3-4, "For my life is spent with sorrow and my years with sighing; My strength has failed because of my iniquity, and my body has wasted away. When I kept silent about my sin, my body wasted away through my groaning all day long. For day and night Thy hand was heavy upon me; my vitality was drained away as with the fever heat of summer." When you carry the weight of unforgiven sin, you can keep walking but you walk with a limp.

4-It disrupts your relationship with God. Although your salvation will not be lost, (your spiritual "DNA" remains intact), your intimacy with God will be stifled.

The devil understands all of these things. His desire is to hurt God, and by hurting God's child he knows he reaches the heart of God. Numbers 32:23 reminds us, "...be sure your sin will find you out." Because he knows the damage revealing your "secret" sin can do, the devil will do his best to expose your sin to the world. His motive is to render you ineffective for the Lord's work by destroying your testimony before a watching world. God will convict you of the sin you are involved in. The Lord's motivation is entirely different. He will convict you in order to change your behavior and grow your character and faith. The devil wants to destroy you while God wants to develop you.

Years ago, while driving in a rough part of town, my eyes caught the marquee of a "gentlemen's club." That's the place where men who aren't considered gentlemen go. I'm not really sure what the sign said, but I remember my mind wandering to thoughts about what went on inside that place. As I continued to stare at the sign, I paid less attention to the road. That's when I hit a deep pot hole. It jarred me back to my senses and moved my mind away from that place. That's the difference between the way God gets our attention and the way the devil seeks to destroy us and all we hold dear. God jolts us back to the good path with a pot hole. The devil puts cars, trucks, utility poles, and buildings in our way. God brings us back through conviction that leads to repentance while the devil brings condemnation that leads to destruction.

Though we might be able to grasp His forgiveness of our sins, we may struggle with embracing how a holy God can forgive the sins of some others.

Some of us have a problem with the entire area of forgiveness. Though we might be able to grasp His forgiveness of our sins, we may struggle with embracing how a holy God can forgive the sins of some others. This problem comes about because we have "humanized" God and made Him into our image. We reshape him into our mold so that we believe He thinks and acts as we do. When we do that, we have trouble believing that God can forgive the likes of Ted Bundy, Timothy McVeigh, Jeffrey Dahmer, Saddam Hussein, Osama Bin Laden, and countless others.

We struggle with this because we are imbalanced in our thinking about God. We only see the holy side of God which brings about judgment and we fail to see the loving side of God that is expressed in grace. When we do that, we tend to see our sin as "not that bad" therefore falling on the grace side of the equation, while we view others' sin as monumental and naturally landing on the side of judgment. But the fact is, God's grace overrides His judgment both for us and for the darkest violator of His law. James 2:13 says. "…mercy triumphs over judgment." That holds true for you, me, and everyone else who will come to Him for forgiveness.

Forgiveness Steps:

Should someone sin against you and desire forgiveness, there would understandably be aspects of that request that you would expect. Forgiveness is not granted simply because it is glibly requested. Likewise, in order to be forgiven by God, certain criteria or attitudes must be in place which demonstrate desire and sincerity.

A-Be Honest. Stop playing games with your sin. Call it what it is; admit the fault. And as a child of the king approach the throne of God's grace.

B-Be Early. Don't let your sins linger and fester. As soon as you recognize sin in your life, deal with it by way of confession and repentance. Confession should come right on the heels of the violation.

C-Be Humble. Remember, you are the one in violation. It is you who sinned against Almighty God. You are the one who is need of forgiveness. This brings to mind that old revival song, "Not my brother, not my sister, but it's me O Lord, standing in the need of prayer." While talking to a friend of mine, he brought up the topic of his dear friend who died while still very young. My friend was angry and resentful. He informed me that when he got to heaven, God had a lot of explaining to do. How arrogant! How proud! How confused! My friend is in for a very rude awakening. When you meet God face to face, it will not be Him who needs to make an explanation; it will be us. We are the ones who have a lot of explaining to do. But mostly we will look on His majesty, bend at the knee and the waist and go completely silent. James 4:6 says, "God is opposed to the proud, but gives grace to the humble."

D-Be Specific. Stop swimming in generalities and name the sin. A blanket drive-by request lacks sincerity. While in a prayer circle one night a man spoke up in prayer and made several requests. His requests were specific and urgent. He was a regular attender to this prayer meeting and always ended his list with the phrase, "And forgive us for our many sins." One night in that circle, just as he finished this well-known phrase, one of the others jumped in and said, "Like what?" The circle became quiet as this question sank in. Moments later the next person started praying and we continued praying until the conclusion. But the message came through. You sinned specifically God wants to hear it specifically. It carries with it a heart of sincerity when you take time to list your offenses.

E-Be Repentant. Repentance is a military term which simply means "about face." In other words, you were heading in one direction, and your desire is to head in the opposite direction, away from the sin. Repentance carries with it a desire not to do it again. Part of your prayer could be a request for empowerment not to have the desire to commit the sin again.

Joel 2:13 instructs us, "Rand rend your heart and not your garments. Now return to the Lord your God, for He is gracious and compassionate, slow to anger and abounding in loving-kindness, and relenting of evil."

From this text it is easy to see that there are two different displays of repentance. One kind of repentance is outward and the other kind is inward. Rending our hearts is personal and is only recognized by

God. Rending our garments is external and is seen by all who are in our presence. How do you know which one to do? It depends on the offense. If the offense is public, then the response should be public. Someone said that public repentance should be as notorious as the public sin. If the offense is private, then the repentance should be the same.

F-Be Consistent. You must constantly seek to keep a clean slate. Asking God to show you what sins you have committed is perfectly acceptable and shows a deep desire to run a race unencumbered by sins which would naturally trip you up. David prayed, "Search me, O God, and know my heart; Try me and know my anxious thoughts; And see if there be any hurtful way in me. And lead me in the everlasting way." (Ps. 139: 23-24).

When we are in need of forgiveness from another person, forgiveness will be granted only at the hands of the offended person. It's up to them to forgive. When someone has sinned against you, it is up to you to forgive. However, as a follower of Christ, it is not optional. As was mentioned earlier, your forgiveness from the Father is contingent on your forgiveness of others. You never know how far forgiveness will go or what impact it will have on others.

Deep in one of Siberia's prison camps a Jew by the name of Dr. Boris Kornfeld was imprisoned. As a medical doctor he worked in surgery and otherwise helped both the staff and the prisoners. He met a Christian, whose name is unknown, whose quiet faith and frequent reciting of the Lord's Prayer moved Dr. Kornfeld.

One day, while repairing a guard's artery which had been cut in a knifing, he seriously considered suturing it in such a way that it would cause him to bleed to death a little while later. Then, appalled by the hatred and violence he saw in his own heart, he found himself repeating the words of the nameless prisoner: "Forgive us our sins as we forgive those who sin against us."

Shortly after that prayer Dr. Kornfeld began to refuse to go along with some of the standard practices of the prison camp, including one day turning in an orderly who had stolen food from a dying patient. After that he knew his life was in danger, so he began to spend as much time as possible in the relative safety of the hospital.

One afternoon he examined a patient who had just been operated on for cancer of the intestines, a man whose eyes and face reflected a depth of spiritual misery and emptiness that moved Kornfeld. So the doctor began to talk to the patient, telling him the entire story, an incredible confession of secret faith.

That night someone snuck in and smashed Dr. Kornfeld's head while he was asleep-he died a few hours later. But Kornfeld's testimony did not die. The patient who had heard his confession became a Christian as a result and he survived that prison camp and went on to tell the world what he had learned there. The patient was the great writer-Aleksandr Solzhenitsyn

Forgiving Yourself:

One of the most difficult aspects of forgiveness has to do with forgiving yourself. Failure to experience personal forgiveness can be crippling and prevent you from moving on in the Christian life. You can't believe you did this or said that. In fact, this particular aspect of the Christian life may be so difficult to achieve, that some people even sabotage their lives because they feel that after what they did, they don't deserve to be happy or successful. This is nothing more than a lack of faith in God and an elevation of self-importance.

Failure to experience personal forgiveness can be crippling and prevent you from moving on in the Christian life.

If you have confessed and repented of your sin, then by the authority of the word of God, you are forgiven. It's not easy, but not to forgive yourself places you above God. After all, if He can forgive you, who are you not to receive that forgiveness and carry the offense with you?

Robert Robinson was a gifted preacher and hymn writer during the eighteenth century. But somehow, he began to drift from the faith and eventually found himself indulging in sin in France. One night, while riding in a carriage in Paris he found himself in the company of a Parisian socialite who had come to Christ. She was reading some poetry aloud, "Come thou fount of every blessing, tune my heart to sing thy grace, streams of mercy never failing, call for hymns of loudest praise."

Immediately Robinson recognized the writing as his own and burst forth in tears. He exclaimed, "I've drifted away and can't find my way back." The woman explained, "Streams of mercy never ceasing. They flow in Paris tonight."

With those words he repented of his sin and recommitted his life to Christ.

On our own, pardon is impossible and we are sentenced to carry the weight of our sin. But in Christ we are forgiven and it is impossible to carry the weight of our sin.

YOU CAN BE FORGIVEN!

SHARING PIECES:

What are some of the roadblocks people have that stop them from experiencing forgiveness?

Share a time when you've "wandered from God." What led to that? How did you restore your relationship?

What role do feelings play in forgiveness?

PRINCIPLE #4
YOU CAN EXERCISE OPTIONS

"IN THE END, IT IS IMPORTANT TO REMEMBER THAT WE CANNOT BECOME WHAT WE NEED TO BE BY REMAINING WHAT WE ARE." -MAX DEPREE

My exercise of choice is bike riding. There's nothing like donning a helmet and glasses and pressing down hard to get rolling. You can fight the hills, coast, or just spin for a while. But in order to really enjoy the trip certain things have to be in place. You've got to have:

» The right bike. If the size is wrong, you'll struggle the entire way.

» The right equipment-that means gears, brakes, and a comfortable seat.

» The right day/conditions. If it's a little cold outside, it's a lot colder on a bike. There's no point in even mentioning ice, snow, or rain.

» The right route. If the terrain is bad, the ride is bad.

» The right destination. It's no fun getting lost, especially if your ten-mile ride turns into a fifteen or twenty-mile ride.

» The right company. When riding with others, it really helps when you're with those who are in approximately the same physical condition that you're in. Waiting for others to catch up or feeling like an anchor to the group is no fun.

These are all choices you have to make before you begin your trip. Any one of them that isn't a good fit can cause your ride to quickly become drudgery.

Life is like that too. In fact, the choices you make today determine the opportunities you have tomorrow. So it is incumbent on us to make good choices as they present themselves to us.

A local high school athlete was recently dismissed from the team. He was involved with drugs and alcohol, clear violations of team rules. Later it was learned that his girlfriend was pregnant. He now has to quit school, go to a rehab center, and get a full-time job to support his child. His pursuit of pleasure cost him a high school diploma, the experiences of athletics, and freedom to be and do so much more.

Proverbs 22:1-3 addresses this. "A good name is to be more desired than great riches, favor is better than silver and gold. The rich and the poor have a common bond, the Lord is the maker of them all. The prudent sees the evil and hides himself, but the naive go on, and are punished for it."

The Psalmist is telling us that when a choice has to be made between a good name (reputation) and wealth, choose a good name. It is possible to have both, but he's simply comparing one to the other.

Recently, a member of the athletic program at a well-known university was released after she was arrested on charges of possession of marijuana with the intent to distribute. She lost her job and reputation because of her pursuit of money.

So what is your reputation? What do people say about you? What is your choice-the favor of God or the pursuit of silver? It all comes to this: God is your maker. He is the one we answer to. We all have a choice-We can choose the world and all it has to offer, or we can choose God and all He has to offer.

I have a sign in our game-room: "The reason people fail most often is that they trade what they want most for what they want at the moment."

A teacher in a nearby school district is finding this out. She was the cheerleading coach. Because she got into some personal financial trouble, she *borrowed* some money from the cheerleading account. It was discovered when she paid it back, and although she kept her teaching job, she was dismissed from her coaching position. Just a few months later she was fired from her teaching job because she was caught having sex with one of her students.

All that speaks to what the Psalmist is saying. A prudent person recognizes evil choices and keeps himself from them. He sees the cliff, knows of the danger, and stays away from it. He understands that it is better to build a fence at the top of the mountain than a hospital at the bottom.

What leads people to make the wrong choices?

There are three major contributing factors to wrong decision making:

1-Using emotions as a guide. When people make decisions with emotions as their guide they are setting themselves up for trouble. Emotions can change drastically. What's appealing today may not be so tomorrow. But when the emotions fade you are left with the decision you've made.

This is readily seen in the purchase of a car at a dealership. When someone becomes emotionally attached to a particular vehicle, he is playing right into the salesperson's hands. The percentage of people who buy increases steadily as the time with the car goes up. Going to the dealership, test-driving, calling, asking questions, returning again, and taking the car home for the weekend are all indicators of an increasing chance of the sale. Why is that? It is because you are creating an emotional bond with the car. You see yourself in the car and buy into the idea that if you don't buy right now, you'll miss out on a great car and a great bargain.

Wisdom is what keeps you from making mistakes. Mistakes, however, are a means to wisdom.

This is true on the moral level as well as the financial level. The difficulty with making good and bad choices on the moral level is this: when you make a good moral choice, there generally are bad immediate results but good long-term results. When you make a bad moral choice, there generally are good immediate results and bad long-term results.

If a young person chooses to go out with friends who are drinking and driving, he is immediately accepted and experiences good short-term results. If they wreck he experiences bad long-term effects. The converse is true as well. If he refuses to go, he is shunned and faces short-term negative effects. If they wreck and he is not in the car, he realizes long-term positive effects.

This is a very difficult concept for young people to grasp. This is due partly to the fact that the reasoning part of their brains is not fully formed until somewhere between the ages of twenty- three and twenty-six. This is also due to the difficulty they have in looking down the road and seeing the big picture. There is something right in front of them keeping them from seeing beyond the weekend. And that something often times is a mirror.

This is why Solomon says in Proverbs 4:23, "Watch over your heart with all diligence, for from it flow the springs of life." Your emotions can lead you in a direction you never wanted your life to go.

2-Lack of Wisdom. It may seem quite obvious to mention this, but there are some nuances regarding wisdom that need to be emphasized. Wisdom is what keeps you from making mistakes. Mistakes, however, are a means to wisdom. You learn to be wise from the experience you gain from mistakes. *But* you don't have to be the one making the mistakes.

A fool is easily recognized. He is constantly making the same mistakes over and over again. He always seems to be bruised, beaten, and broke. He goes again and again into the same situations and always comes out on the losing end of the stick. In contrast, a smart person is one who makes a mistake, learns from it, and avoids the same decision that brought him the trouble in the first place. In further contrast, a truly wise person is one who studies a situation, asks questions of others, and learns from the mistakes *of others*. He sees the holes that others have fallen into and walks around them. This is what the writer was talking about in Proverbs 11:14, "Where there is no guidance the people fall, but in abundance of counselors there is victory."

Wisdom gives you the long view. It keeps you out of trouble, debt, and pain. It helps you measure your options against those who have traveled down the road you're on. Because the natural tendency is to become what you surround yourself with, those who keep company with wise people find themselves becoming wise.

The difference is seen in "Autobiography in Five Short Chapters "by Portia Nelson.

(There's a hole in My Sidewalk)

Chapter 1

I walk down the street.

There is a deep hole in the sidewalk.

I fall in.

I am lost ... I am helpless.

It isn't my fault.

It takes forever to find a way out.

Chapter 2

I walk down the same street.

There is a deep hole in the sidewalk.

I pretend I don't see it.

I fall in again.

I can't believe I am in the same place.

But it isn't my fault.

It still takes a long time to get out.

Chapter 3

I walk down the same street.

There is a deep hole in the sidewalk.

I see it is there.

I still fall in ... it's a habit.

My eyes are open.

I know where I am.

It is my fault.

I get out immediately.

Chapter 4

I walk down the same street.

There is a deep hole in the sidewalk.

I walk around it.

Chapter 5

I walk down another street.

3-Lack of Experience. On the heels of not having wisdom is the problem that comes from not having experience. Experience helps you learn your limitations. This is true from a financial, relational, or physical standpoint. The help you get from experience is like the fence that keeps you from going over the edge and becoming hurt by life.

Motorcyclists are involved in a lot of a lot of avoidable accidents simply because their lack of experience causes them to expect the bike to do things it was not meant to do. They do things beyond the limitations of the bike or the rider such as: going too fast, turning on gravel, riding too close, or riding in poor conditions. Each of these can lead to an accident they never saw coming. Experienced bikers know what their bike is meant to do and what it's not meant to do. They tend to look way ahead and see the danger out in front of them. They learn from others' mistakes and avoid situations that would put them at risk of an accident. That is how you have to view life. You must learn from others' mistakes and look way down the road to avoid the trouble others have experienced. Life is determined by choices.

Making the right choice tends to bring about good results.

Of course, there are few guarantees in life, but the tendencies still exist. The "if/then" principle of life is still intact:

» *If* you choose to get a degree, *then* you stand a better chance at getting a job.

» *If* you work hard, *then* you are in a better position to make more money.

» *If* you stay out of debt (through resisting the temptation to buy toys and the discipline of deferred gratification), *then* you will have the freedom to do some of the things you always wanted to do.

» *If* you choose not to compromise your faith, *then* you can live your life in confidence and assurance of God enacting His plan for you.

As we've seen in Proverbs 22:3, the prudent person sees the evil and avoids it. He has parameters, builds defenses, and invites accountability. Contrary to popular belief, freedom comes from self-discipline. This is true physically, financially, and spiritually. The person who avoids evil also sidesteps the negative consequences evil brings with it. Behind each enticement of ungodly pleasure there is a hidden consequence that is embraced by the offender. Committing adultery brings with it the possibility of divorce, disease, and an unplanned pregnancy. Taking drugs leads to addiction. Stealing leads to imprisonment. Lying leads to mistrust and a loss of friends. Avoiding evil requires a person to take the long view regarding decisions.

Joseph understood this. In Genesis 37-46 we find his story. He is a shepherd of his father's sheep, is promised by God through a dream to be a ruler, is enslaved, sent to jail, and becomes the second in command of all of Egypt. In Genesis 39 Joseph is serving as a slave in Potiphar's house. So far in his life nothing is working out well. The dreams he's had have not even come close to being fulfilled. He's been taken away from his family, sold by his brothers, given to the highest bidder, and assigned duties serving in the house of Potiphar.

While there, Potiphar's wife makes a move on him. The house is empty. No doubt she is beautiful since Potiphar could choose any woman he wanted. He was alone with this good-looking woman. She made a direct plea for him to sleep with her.

The world was saying, "go for it!" "You deserve it!" "If it feels good, do it!" And the ever popular, "Everybody's doing it!" I'm sure that Joseph must have entertained those thoughts and many others. He may have even been thinking that this was his big break, a chance to finally have some pleasure in his life.

But Joseph knew the consequences of bad choices. He knew that in spite of his lowly position he was still God's man and that God had a great plan for his life. He saw the evil and resisted it. His response was, "Behold, with me here, my master does not concern himself with anything in the house, and he has put all that he owns in my charge. There is no one greater in this house than I, and he has withheld nothing from me except you because you are his wife. How then could I do this great evil and sin against God." (Genesis 39:8-9).

In I Samuel 2:30 God reminds us, "...for those who honor me, I will honor, and those who despise Me will be lightly esteemed." Joseph knew, understood, and adhered to this concept, and it kept him out of trouble. It ultimately led him into leadership over the nation of Egypt. Life is determined by choices and making the right choices tends to bring about good results.

Likewise, **making the wrong choices tends to bring about bad results**. In II Kings 5 we find the story of Naaman. But along with his story, we read a sub-story about Elisha's servant Gehazi. Naaman was captain of the army of Aram. He was an accomplished leader but was a leper. He comes to Elisha for healing and Elisha heals him. When he wants to reward the man of God for his service, Elisha refuses and sends him on his way a new man. Elisha's servant Gehazi sees the opportunity for gain and runs after the company of Naaman. Gehazi lies and says that Elisha sent him and needs money and clothes for a couple of young men who are the sons of prophets. Naaman is more than happy to oblige and gives him what he needs.

When he returns to Elisha, Gehazi lies to a *prophet*, about where he's been is found out and becomes a leper for the rest of his life. Choosing to lie, deceive, and take what isn't rightfully yours and ending up a leper who is ostracized from all of society--not a great outcome for a little silver and a couple of changes of clothes. As the Scripture says, "The rich and the poor" (Naaman and Gehazi), "have a common bond, the Lord is the maker of them all." And since God is the maker, He orchestrates what goes on in the affairs of men.

Heroism isn't just for those who wear capes.

In dealing with so many men, I've found that there are some commonalities men have regarding their desires. The most prevalent four I've discovered:

1. Men want to be admired. Men buy things, get close to people, gain titles or try to look a certain way in order to impress those who will slow down long enough to notice.

2. Men want to be heroes. Along with wanting to be admired, men have an insatiable desire to be somebody's hero. It could be through sports, special discoveries, or that grandchild that they continually rescue from trouble. Men are enamored by their abilities and their accomplishments. Trophies matter to men and they hold on to them like a bulldog holds on to a bone.

3. Men want to give themselves to something that will outlive them. They desire to be involved in something noble, a worthy cause or event. They dive into anything as long as there is a challenge connected to it.

4. Men want to know that they matter. They want to be difference makers and understand that they can contribute something worthwhile to a project. Here is where many men get confused. They confuse affluence with influence. They obviously are not the same. Too many think that just because they have possessions they have a right to have their voice heard above the rest. But men in general want to know that they count for something.

Each of these desires can be found in living out a personal relationship with Christ. When a person is living the Christian faith consistently and sincerely, he finds himself admired by those around him.

Do you want to be a hero? Go meet the needs of those who can't take care of themselves. Scoop up some young people and pour your life into them. Invest in other's lives and give your time and energy to them. Heroism isn't just for those who wear capes. Can you name something that is more noble that a life found in Christ? Passing on the gospel of Jesus Christ is the highest calling a person can aspire to. Who can matter more than the person who is sharing the good news that will lead a person to live with God forever? When God calls you to be His servant, don't stoop to be a king.

A few years ago, a friend of mine took me up in his plane. It was a cub with a seating arrangement one behind the other. It was a beautiful day and we took off from the grass field without incident. After flying for a while he let me take over the controls and handle the plane by myself. All of that is right up my alley. I was having a great time. But then I noticed that the ride began to get more and more bumpy. The plane began to shake and pitch. A couple of times the wind really grabbed hold of us and startled me. I asked him why that was happening and he explained that we were heading into a front that was moving in. At that point he said, "I got it." And he took over the controls. Can you guess what I did? I let him. My friend is a commercial pilot and he knows exactly what he's doing. Turning loose of the controls was not something I debated for a moment. It was the right choice.

Turning over the controls of your life to the creator and architect takes very little mental effort. He's got our best interest at heart and wants better things for us than we want for ourselves. Life offers options; where you spend eternity is one of them.

SHARING PIECES:

Name a time when you made a decision based on emotions. What was the outcome?

Who do you consider the wisest person you know personally?

Share a personal if/then scenario.

What is the worst decision you've ever made in your life?

PRINCIPLE #5
YOU CAN ENJOY FORGIVENESS

"WE ARE MOST LIKE BEASTS WHEN WE KILL. WE ARE MOST LIKE MEN WHEN WE JUDGE.WE ARE MOST LIKE GOD WHEN WE FORGIVE." -UNKNOWN

When my friend Bill was in college and attending summer classes, he lived in a lake house with a well-to-do doctor. The doctor let him have the run of the place and Bill was more than happy to fill that role. While the doctor and his wife were away on vacation Bill took the opportunity to invite his friend Mike over. They were planning on spending the day on the lake in the doctor's ski boat. As luck would have it, Mike invited a couple of girls and before long the four of them were heading to the dock for a great time on the lake. Wanting to impress the girls, Bill popped the throttle and off they went. Bill was surprised at the lack of speed the boat had and gave it some more gas. Still the boat chugged along. He went to check the engine when he noticed a good section of the dock floating behind the boat. Failure to untie from the dock can really slow you down.

As long as you have unforgiveness dragging behind you, you'll find yourself in a sluggish state at best.

It can be the same way with unforgiveness. You can move through life, but you can't make the progress you'd like to. As long as you have unforgiveness dragging behind you, you'll find yourself in a sluggish state at best. You've got to cut the rope that has been holding you back for so long.

Several medical and psychological studies have revealed that people who forgive:

» Have a better immune system and lower blood pressure.

» Experience better mental health.

» Feel better physically.

» Experience lower amounts of anger and few symptoms of anxiety and depression.

» Tend to maintain more satisfying and long-lasting relationships.

Previously, we've covered paternal forgiveness. That is the vertical dimension of forgiveness. Here, we will talk about personal forgiveness. That is the horizontal dimension.

Forgiveness runs counter to our flesh. It is not natural and can seem insurmountable. When you examine withholding forgiveness, you'll find that pride is at the headwaters. "Who do they think they are?" "Don't they know who I am?" "They have no right to treat me this way!"

The mind of the flesh calls us to lust, greed, pride, self-righteousness, anger, selfishness, and a host of other sins. It leads to emotional, physical, social, and psychological destruction. But the mind of Christ calls us to love, forgiveness, faith, truth, compassion, wisdom, and sacrifice. This leads to emotional, physical, social, and psychological healing.

Further, as we've already seen, my forgiveness from God is contingent on my forgiving others. Jesus said in Mark 11:25, "And whenever you stand praying, forgive, if you have anything against anyone; so that your Father also who is in heaven may forgive you your transgressions." Also, In Luke 6:37 He says, "And do not judge and you will not be judged; and do not condemn and you will not be condemned; pardon, and you will be pardoned."

The cry of our hearts is, "But you don't know what they did to me!" No, I don't. But I've seen others hurt and I've watched them go through the entire process and reach the point of forgiveness and I've seen the healing take place in their lives.

From an emotional standpoint, when we are wronged, we have an opportunity to descend in our emotions toward that person. At each level, there is an emotional exit door called forgiveness that we may use. We start out with awareness. This is where we evaluate the wrong done to us (and where our pride measures the offense). If the offense warrants it, we get upset. We may pout and dwell on it. Next we move to the level of getting mad. Usually this is where we vent to the person and more often, to our friends. Of course they only hear our side of the story and many times it's colored with our perspective. Then we move to anger. This is where it really gets personal and we have difficulty letting it go. Retribution kicks in and we feel that we must repay the person for the sin against us. The next stage involves resentment. We analyze someone's life and decide what should happen to that person. If we hear that something good has taken place we immediately label it unfair and only see bad things as a possibility. The next stage is bitterness. The very name brings us all sorts of negative connotations. We may even fantasize about someone's undoing and even death. The final stage is all out hatred. We make plans to undermine their lives and may even follow through with inflicting pain or death.

When you witness someone granting forgiveness in any area where your flesh would deem it unwarranted, there is a tendency to pause over it in admiration. You find it remarkable. The word of God is replete with examples of forgiveness. David forgave his son Absalom. Esau forgave Jacob. Joseph forgave his brothers. And Jesus forgives everybody, even those who put Him on the cross. Life too is filled with examples of people who found the strength to forgive even the most heinous of sins.

When you witness someone granting forgiveness in any area where your flesh would deem it unwarranted, there is a tendency to pause over it in admiration. You find it remarkable.

Rebecca Nichols Alonzo tells the story of being a young girl and watching from under a table as a man entered their home and shot her mother to death and seriously wounded her father. The man was convicted and spent several years in jail. When released, she and her brother were united with him and without his asking, extended complete and total forgiveness. They even presented him with a Bible. Agreement on the sin was universal. Forgiveness or hatred were the options. She and her brother chose forgiveness-total and complete.

The truth is justice cannot heal; only forgiveness can. People all over the country gather together for various occasions and sing "Amazing Grace." I have yet to hear any person or group of people sing "Amazing Justice." We don't always have the authority to pardon an offense but we always have the command to forgive an offense.

Some offenses are small and the road to forgiveness is short. But some are such major chasms that crossing seems impossible.

When forgiveness is withheld, it carries with it lasting affects. It hurts our spirits, our relationship with God, and our relationship with another person. It may even be the barrier to someone else's relationship with God.

When our friend Pam was in high school she was on a date with her boyfriend. Later that evening they found themselves in a secluded romantic spot overlooking a lake. While there, a man knocked on the window asking for help. He told them his car was broken down and he needed a ride. When her boyfriend opened the door, the man hit him over the head knocking him out. He tied him up in the back seat and drove away with Pam in the front. He stated that he would kill her boyfriend if she didn't cooperate. He drove off to a more secluded place and over the next several hours raped her repeatedly. How horrific! How does anyone ever recover from that?

Through the grace of God, Pam found a way to forgive that man. She has recovered and uses that episode in her testimony to help others overcome the sins committed against them. Her story is nothing short of inspirational. She understands what Paul meant when he wrote in Romans 12:21, "Do not be overcome by evil, but overcome evil with good."

Her old boyfriend's story doesn't end the same way. He never brought himself to the point where he could forgive that man. His bitterness has burned a hole into the depths of his soul. He's struggled with drugs, alcohol, divorce, and abuse. Someone has rightly said, "Bitterness is drinking poison and waiting for the other person to die." He understands that full well!

How is it possible to forgive? Some offenses are small and the road to forgiveness is short. But some are such major chasms that crossing seems impossible. How can I forgive? There are several things that must be done in order to be in a mental, emotional, and spiritual position to forgive these deep hurts.

» You must pray for the strength to forgive. Some even have to pray for the desire to pray for the strength to forgive.

» You have to establish an understanding that you have no right *not* to forgive. As a follower of Christ, you are crucified with Him. Galatians 2:20 tells us, "I have been crucified with Christ; and it is no longer I who live, but Christ lives in me; and the life which I now live in the flesh I live by faith, in the Son of God, who loved me, and delivered Himself up for me." As a person who has been crucified, you have two things in common with all others who recognize they are crucified: they have no plans of their own and they cannot look behind them. If you belong to Christ, you cannot have plans not to forgive and you cannot look behind you to review the offense.

» You must put the offense in perspective. Are you without sin? Have you never offended anyone? Are you in position to cast stones? Wasn't it your transgressions that sent Christ to the cross? Yet you've been forgiven. Aren't you compelled to forgive? Jesus tried to drive this point home with a very familiar parable named the unforgiving debtor. It's found in Matthew 18. In short, it's about one person being forgiven a great debt but upon receiving his freedom demanding another person pay a much smaller debt. How many of us are holding onto the minor sins others have committed against us while ignoring the great sins we've committed against others and even God?

» Be realistic about the offense. We have a natural tendency to think that any offense against us is bigger than whatever sin we may have committed against someone else. Further, we also default to what can be called "a kitchen sink" argument. We pile up any transgressions others have committed and lump them all into the one at hand. On top of that we suffer from beguilement. To be beguiled is to have layers of false thinking piled on top of the truth so high that we struggle to get to the truth. For instance: If we call a friend and ask him to return our call and don't hear from him, we call again. After not hearing from him we may call again. At this point we are irritated by the lack of attention. Then we start to reason, "Maybe he is mad at me." "Maybe he is not that good a friend after all." "Maybe that sarcastic comment he made at the party last week meant more than I thought." "You know, I don't think he ever liked me. He's just another phony person and I don't really need him in my life anyway."

But what is the truth? He didn't return your phone call. But the beguiling brought you from the fact that he didn't return your call to the conclusion, "I don't really need him in my life anyway." Then later you are embarrassed when the truth comes out. He was on vacation and never got your phone call. Be realistic about what you label a sin.

» Be determined to forgive. Forgiveness is a choice just like love, hate, and the rest of our emotions. You have got to make up your mind that you will forgive. Then you work through the process to make it happen.

» Put it behind you. Honestly forgive. Never bring it up, dig it up, or cast a line for it again. Bury it and relinquish your rights to it. In her book *Hurt People Hurt People*, Dr. Sandra D. Wilson states, "Remember, forgiving is not denying the wrong they did; it's releasing the right to wrong them in return." If you bury it deep enough, you will struggle to bring it up again.

I was wrestling with this issue several years back. I decided that I would freely and willfully forgive anyone who had done an injustice to me at any time in my life. So I sat at my desk and let my mind wander to the past. I thought of all the violations against me, labeled them sins, and wrote them down. The list was long. It included big and small things and names and incidents that had long lay dormant. Among them:

-A teacher in first grade who brought me in front of the class and put gum on my nose. I was so embarrassed that I cried. This led to further embarrassment.

-The old man who kissed me on the lips when he gave me a ride home when I was ten.

-The guy who "sucker punched" me in seventh grade and then continued to hit me until I was nearly unconscious. We're facebook friends today.

-The woman who broke my heart a few months before our wedding.

-The man who lied about me and almost cost me my job.

-The guys on the coaching staff who ostracized me because I didn't believe or act like they did.

-My fraternity brother who publicly humiliated me about my faith.

The list goes on and on. Big sins and little sins, some of which you may label as inconsequential, while others you may think are justified in withholding forgiveness. I put all of these on a legal pad and went to the altar alone. I talked to God about each of these and asked Him for the strength to forgive. I left no stone unturned and covered everything regarding each situation. I also asked for forgiveness where I reacted in a sinful way. It took a very long time, but I cleared the air with everyone from my past and came away from that altar so much lighter for the experience.

On the way out of the sanctuary, I made a stop in the restroom. I took each of the sheets filled with sins, tore them up, and flushed them down the toilet. Those sins are forgiven and it is absolutely impossible for them to be retrieved.

» If possible, tell the other person you forgave him. Though this is not a pre-requisite for forgiveness, it may open the door for healing, restoration, and reconciliation. Reconciliation is of great benefit but is not necessarily a part of forgiveness. In fact, it may be impossible to be reconciled with someone. The person may have died or be unwilling. But forgiveness is always possible. While we cannot always bring reconciliation, forgiveness is always within our power to grant.

» Exercise your forgiveness. Forgiveness has various levels to it. More times than I care to recount, I hear people say, "I'll forgive them but I won't forget it." That's code for "I'm not really going to forgive, I'll just go through the motions." This is level-one forgiveness. I call it, "Historical forgiveness." That means that on the surface I'll forgive, but I'll always keep the offense in mind and use it as a weapon when it's convenient. Forgiveness doesn't mean you're forgetting. We may not have the capacity for that. But it does mean that you are going to act like you have forgiven. Level-two forgiveness is called, "Practical" forgiveness. It means that I genuinely forgive the person, but the offense is in my heart or head and I avoid this person at all costs. Essentially, he is dead to me. "Spiritual" or "biblical" forgiveness is level-three forgiveness. It is the type of forgiveness that is very difficult but essential in the life of the Christian. Jesus put it this way, "But I say to you who hear, love your enemies, do good to those who hate you, bless those who curse you, pray for those who mistreat you." (Luke 6:27-28).

This calls you to be pro-active in your forgiveness. It means you have to invest in that person. You have to honor him, pray for him, be kind to him, help him, and generally display the heart of Christ in all your dealings with him. I'm not saying that it will be easy, but I can promise you the experience of true freedom.

In the days of the Revolutionary War there lived in Ephrata, Pennsylvania, Peter Miller, a Baptist pastor who enjoyed the friendship of

General Washington. There also dwelt in that town one Michael Wittman, an evil-minded man who did all in his power to abuse and oppose this pastor. One day Michael Wittman was involved in treason and was arrested and sentenced to death. The old preacher started out on foot and walked the whole seventy miles to Philadelphia to plead for this man's life. He was admitted into Washington's presence and at once begged for the life of the traitor. Washington said, "No, Peter, I cannot grant you the life of your friend." The preacher exclaimed, "He is not my friend-he is the bitterest of enemy I have." Washington cried, "What? You've walked seventy miles to save the life of an enemy? That puts the matter in a different light. I will grant the pardon." And he did. And Peter Miller took Michael Wittman from the very shadow of death back to his own home in Ephrata-no longer as an enemy, but as a friend.

"Humanity is never so beautiful as when praying for forgiveness or else forgiving another." -Jean Paul Richter

Jean Paul Richter says, "Humanity is never so beautiful as when praying for forgiveness or else forgiving another." This is seen in the story of two brothers who owned adjoining farms. They lived side by side for forty years. One day, they had a small disagreement. This led to a major difference and an exchange of bitter words. It ended in months of angry silence. Soon, a man came by with his carpenter's box looking for work. One of the brothers hired him to build a tall fence by the creek between the two properties. The man set to work, but instead of building a fence, he built a bridge. When the man who hired him came out to address the carpenter he found his brother coming across the bridge to meet him. The two apologized and mended their relationship. They embraced and invited the carpenter to lunch. He declined saying, "I can't stay. I have many other bridges to build."

Do you have any bridges you need to build or have you been busy building fences between you and others? If you're interested in building bridges, forgiveness makes great material for construction, and the bridge can always be labeled "Peace."

SHARING PIECES:

What is your earliest memory of an instance in which you were hurt?

What would you say is the biggest barrier to forgiveness?

Have you been to Christ for forgiveness? What happened?

Besides Christ, what is the biggest story you've ever heard about a person offering forgiveness?

PRINCIPLE #6
YOU CAN MAKE A DIFFERENCE

"CARVE YOUR NAME ON HEARTS AND NOT ON MARBLE."
-CHARLES H. SPURGEON

It's not an uncommon challenge and it usually comes in several parts: Name the U.S. Ambassador to China. Name the number one film in 2000. Name the Chief Editor of the New York Times. Name three generals in the US Army.

The world can't tell you who or what is important in your life; only you can determine this. And the world can't label you insignificant if you strive to make a difference in somebody's life.

My guess is you did pretty poorly in naming any one of the people or things that grab the headlines and are quickly labeled people or things of significance or impact. These are people and things that shape our world and our society. People depend on them. They make huge life changing decisions every day. And yet, so many of us struggle to fill in just one of the blanks. Why is that?

The next question is for you to name a person who helped you during a difficult time. Can you name a teacher or coach you admired? How about a hero you had growing up? Identify your best friend in high school. I have no doubt that you did quite well on the second challenge.

In reality, the world may attach labels to people and things that seem significant and life changing, but if you are not in close personal contact, they carry very little weight in your life. The reality is that it is not things or distant people that have a memorable impact in your life. It's the people you know and things you've experienced that cause you to label them significant. The world can't tell you who or what is important in your life; only you can determine this. And the world can't label you insignificant if you strive to make a difference in somebody's life.

What you'll find is that everyone longs to be significant. Everyone desires to make a contribution. Everyone yearns to be noticed. That's why people paint their names on bridges and boulders in big bold letters. That is the motivation behind body piercing and tattoos. That is why people start so many of their sentences with the words "I, me," or "my." Their entire actions are screaming "Look at me!" "Will somebody please notice me?" "Can't anyone see that I am here?" If you ask the average man to tell you something about himself, he will usually tell you about one and maybe all three of the following things: What he does, what he owns, or who he knows. That is because he has mistakenly concluded that these are the things worth recognizing. These are the things of value and significance. While it is important to realize that things are important, we must understand that it is people who carry significance. Because of this we must commit ourselves to people and not things.

"Appreciation is thanking, recognition is seeing, and encouragement is hope for the future." -Unknown

Paul, in his second letter to Timothy, indirectly points this out. 2 Timothy 1:16-18 says, "The Lord grant mercy to the house of Onesiphorus, for he often refreshed me and was not ashamed of my chains; but when he was in Rome, he eagerly searched for me and found me. The Lord grant to him to find mercy from the Lord on that day-and you know very well what services he rendered at Ephesus." We know very little about this man named Onesiphorus. But in his life and the way he lived it, we find four major factors regarding making a difference in someone's life:

1-People who make a difference are refreshing.

Onesiphorus' name means "profit bearer." Paul notes that he was refreshed by Onesiphorus. It is quite possible that at the time of Paul's writing, he had died. But so impactful was he that Paul felt compelled to write about him and ask the Lord to bless this little known man's family.

So how does one become refreshing? I believe that the most important factor in refreshing someone is to encourage that person. Have you noticed that no one complains of having too much encouragement? Too many trials, too many complaints, too many responsibilities, yes, but never too much encouragement. I have yet to meet a man or a woman who would say, "I know you're trying to encourage me, but I think I've been encouraged enough already. Save your encouragement for someone else." No, we soak up encouragement like a thirsty person soaks up water. We ask for an example or explanation when we receive a compliment. We enter circles where we know the people will speak life into us. Someone has rightly said, "Appreciation is thanking, recognition is seeing, and encouragement is hope for the future."

In 1989 the Christian artists "Newsong" recorded the song "Light Your World." The lyrics speak deeply of the simplicity of encouraging someone else:

Two doors down one rocking chair is rocking.

She sits there all alone, her husband dead and gone.

The best years of her life they spent together.

He was always strong, but now she's on her own.

And the telephone never rings.

No one laughs, no one sings.

It's quiet there.

Does anyone care?

(Chorus) Light your world.
Let the love of God shine through
In the little things you do.
Light your world.
And though your light may be
Reaching only two or three,
Light your world.

A knocking at her door breaks the silence.
She looks out to see a little boy from down the street.
She cracks the door, surprised that he came over.
Flowers in his hand like a little gentleman.
He said, 'I picked these just for you.
I hope you like the color blue.
Could I stay a while?
I love to see you smile.'

Light your world.
Let the love of God shine through
In the little things you do.
Light your world.
And though your light may be
Reaching only two or three,
Light your world.

It only takes a little time

To show someone how much you care.

It only takes a little time

To answer someone's biggest prayer.

I learned this simple lesson very early in my freshman year in college. We started a Christian club on campus. There were a number of students involved and our numbers grew quickly. There was a girl named Maureen who attended early on but did not show up for a couple of weeks. I ran into her in the campus bookstore and mentioned to her that I missed her at our meeting last night. She said thanks and walked away. Two days later she was walking along the sidewalk a few paces in front of me. I was unaware she was there and didn't know she knew I was behind her. Without prompting, she turned around and said, "You know, Steve, that meant so much to me that you would miss me at the other night's meeting. Thank you." Then she turned and kept walking. And here it is decades later and I still remember how easy it was to bring encouragement to someone's heart.

Dr. William Mayo of the Mayo Clinic understands this. After a staff member read a medical research paper at a staff meeting, he later saw him in the elevator. Dr. Mayo put his hand on his shoulder and handing him a note simply said, "Good work." The note read, "Dear Brian, I learned more about liver cancer from that presentation of yours than I ever knew before. It was a good job." You can easily imagine that Brian did not touch the floor for the rest of the day. He was refreshed by that word of encouragement. Mark Twain said, "I can live three months on a good compliment." So can the people we have a chance to encourage.

Hebrews 10:24-25 tells us, "And let us consider how to stimulate one another to love and good deeds, not forsaking our own assembling together, as is the habit of some, but encouraging one another; and all the more, as you see the day drawing near." In other words, figure out different ways to encourage people who are doing good things.

Gather together for the sake of doing good things and encouraging others to continue to be involved in good works.

Elizabeth Harrison said, "Those who are lifting the world upward and onward are those who encourage more than critique." How are you on the encouragement/critique continuum? Do you have some adjustments to make? If you want to make a difference in someone's life, become an encourager. If you give a person a meal, you will meet the needs of the stomach. If you give a person a blanket, you will meet the needs of the body. But if you give a person some encouragement, you will meet the needs of the soul.

2-People who make a difference are not ashamed of the circumstance of others.

Paul was alone and in prison. To be associated with him was to identify with him and to identify with him meant the possibility of the same condemnation he was facing. I have no doubt that Onesiphorus knew that. Yet he went right past all of that and came and sought out his friend Paul.

So often we get hung up on a person's looks, status, history, color, or any number of surface things that keep us away from other people. The Bible instructs us in 2 Corinthians 5:16-18, "Therefore from now on we recognize no man according to the flesh; even though we have known Christ according to the flesh, yet now we know Him this way no longer. Therefore if any man is in Christ, he is a new creature; the old things passed away; behold, new things have come. Now all these things are from God, who reconciled us to Himself through Christ and gave us the ministry of reconciliation."

James Robert Kennedy lives in Anderson, S.C. He is mentally challenged. He was befriended by Harold Jones, the head football coach of T. L. Hanna High School. Their relationship and the subsequent relationship he had with the students and athletic teams were so inspirational that it led to the making of the movie *Radio* (2003). At first the students and town-folk shied away from Radio. They didn't understand him and some were afraid of him. But because of the efforts of Jones, they were able to look past the exterior and arrive at a position where they embraced James. Even though he is much older today, he still is part of the T.L Hanna campus and can be seen at football and basketball games. Coach Jones made a life changing difference in a young man because he was willing to look beyond a person's disability and see a heart that was hurting and just wanted to be loved. This in turn led to members of a school looking after someone who couldn't look after himself. All this was because of one man desiring to make a difference.

Dale Carnegie said, "If we are so contemptibly selfish that we can't radiate a little happiness and pass on a bit of honest appreciation without trying to get something out of the other person in return-if our souls are not bigger than sour crab apples, we shall meet with the failure we so richly deserve."

What is it that's keeping you from getting next to people? What is about them that is preventing you from investing in their lives and having an impact on them? What will it take for you to get over yourself and your pre-conceived notions about people's race, gender, background, struggles, and pain? Whatever it takes, you must push past those issues and determine to make the change in their lives they so desperately need.

The story is told of a hippie who arrived late at church one Sunday morning. He had long hair, dirty clothes, and no shoes. No one greeted him at the door. No one shook his hand. No one made room for him. Most in the congregation quietly wished he'd just go away and not disturb their comfortable little church. Undaunted, the young man walked into the sanctuary and found the only spot available in the entire place. While the congregation sang, he walked all the way to the front and sat down on the floor in front of the altar. What brashness. What disrespect. Someone had to do something. The entire room was nervous. Somebody had to step up and let that man know that his behavior was unacceptable. But who would take the reins and straighten him out? Then it happened. An elderly deacon who was a prominent member of the congregation began walking down the aisle with the help of his cane. Finally someone would do something about that young man. Finally someone would bring him to his senses and quietly let him know he was out of place and should go elsewhere. The entire congregation was fixed on the man walking slowly but purposely down the aisle. Then the unthinkable happened. He hung his cane on the front row pew and slowly lowered himself to the floor to join the young man in worship. What a heart! What a statement! What a difference! People who make a difference are not ashamed of the circumstances of others.

3-People who make a difference extend themselves.

Sometimes making a difference means paying a price. It just might cost you something to be impactful in someone's life. The heroes in movies and stories are those who go farther and give more to something or someone outside themselves.

Jonathan made a difference in the life of David. He was heir to the throne. The kingdom would be his. Yet he stood by his friend David and faced the anger of his father in order to do what was right. The little boy with the five loaves and two fishes (all he had for lunch) gave it to Jesus and became part of a miracle. Isaiah spoke clearly and said, "Here I am Lord, send me!" The woman who owned the expensive perfume poured it all out on the feet of Jesus. It cost her dearly, but she gave what she had and honored the Lord. Because of that act of sacrifice Jesus said of her, "Wherever this gospel is preached to the whole world, what this woman has done will also be spoken of in memory of her."

The best leaders are the ones who serve. They are in the habit of meeting others' needs. They look out for the interests of others rather than their own. They are easy to spot because they are always found doing things for others.

In the case of Onesiphorus, Paul says, "… he eagerly searched for me and found me." Paul was a deserted prisoner. He was kept under constant guard. He was an enemy of Rome. Connecting with him could bring real problems. Yet it did not stop Onesiphorus.

He kept asking. He kept looking. He kept gathering information until he found his friend and ministered to him. He made a difference because he paid a price to make a difference.

4-People who make a difference serve.

The best leaders are the ones who serve. They are in the habit of meeting others' needs. They look out for the interests of others rather than their own. They are easy to spot because they are always found doing things for others.

General Omar Bradley was labeled "the G.I. General." G.I. stands for "government issued." He got that name because he was a leader who was not afraid to get close to those in his command. They identified with him. He was often seen in foxholes talking with the men, giving them cigarettes, and handing them gifts. The men loved him because he was one of them. They knew he cared about them and they knew they could count on him to look out for them. He was the picture of a servant leader.

You can't go far when you're speaking about servant leaders before you come to Jesus. Matthew 20:28 tells us, "…the Son of Man did not come to be served, but to serve, and to give His life a ransom for many." His purpose was to serve, to give, and to be the exchange for the souls who would accept him.

The key phrases used by those who have a heart for serving are:

> "What can I do for you?"
>
> "How can I help you?"
>
> "What do you need?"

They understand the Bible's command in Hebrews 13:16, "And do not neglect doing good and sharing; for with such sacrifices God is pleased"

Life presents each of us with a choice: we can waste it, we can spend it, or we can invest it. The way to go is to invest it and the place to invest it is in things that will last forever. The only two assets we have that are eternal are God's word and people. We must be willing to invest in both. It's not about stuff. It's not about applause. It's not about position. It is about people and the lasting difference we can make in their lives.

The only two assets we have that are eternal are God's word and people.

The decision to make a difference in someone's life has everything to do with how you see your position in life. Some see themselves as owners. Owners don't see others as a priority in their lives. They care about themselves and those who can benefit them. Managers see their roles as controlling what they have and the people around them. But tenants are those who see they have a responsibility to look out for others particularly those who can't look out for themselves and to push them forward to a better stage in life. If you see yourself in the last position, then you'll be able to say without stammering or hesitation, "I can make a difference!"

SHARING PIECES:

Who would you name as a person who has had the most impact on your life?

____

____

____

____

How are you positioning yourself to make a difference in someone's life?

____

____

____

____

What is the biggest price you've paid to invest in someone else?

____

____

____

____

PRINCIPLE #7
YOU CAN BE A WITNESS

"I CAN'T FIND A VERSE IN SCRIPTURE THAT COMMANDS A LOST PERSON TO GO TO CHURCH, BUT I KNOW A LOT OF SCRIPTURE THAT COMMANDS BELIEVERS TO GO INTO A LOST WORLD." -HOWARD HENDRICKS

This is a principle the Devil does not want you to understand, much less embrace. It involves the concept and assurance that you have been empowered and commanded to talk to others about your relationship with Christ and explain to them that they too can have what you have. They can be saved from their sins and assure for themselves a place in the presence of God for all eternity. The methods of becoming a witness for God are as varied as the avenue by which people come to Christ. Some are straightforward while others are highly creative. But all involve responding to the command of God to do it.

Jesus wasn't suggesting we become witnesses and disciple makers. He was commanding it. It is not an option for the Christian.

Matthew 28:18-20 is a passage that is no stranger to many. In fact, it's so universally known among Christians that it has become ignored much like a tree that grows in a field. You know it's there, but you've driven past it so many times that you no longer take notice of it. "And Jesus came up and spoke to them, saying, 'All authority has been given to me in heaven and on earth. Go therefore and make disciples of all the nations, baptizing them in the name of the Father and the Son and the Holy Spirit, teaching them to observe all that I commanded you; and lo, I am with you always, even to the end of the age."

This is known as *the great commission*, but for some of us it has morphed into *the great suggestion*. Somehow we decided that this command (and it is a command) is only meant for those who have a particular "gifting" in the area of evangelism and discipling. Therefore it has become optional much like elective classes offered in college. But Jesus wasn't suggesting we become witnesses and disciple makers. He was commanding it. It is not an option for the Christian. It is our marching orders. And as good soldiers of the cross it is our job to take this command seriously and obediently. We have a command and therefore a responsibility. How we go about fulfilling that command depends on a combination of our personality and the opportunities that present themselves. But be assured of this: Excitement about your relationship with Christ plus a deep commitment to His command plus creativity equals opportunities to share the gospel.

While in college, Jill Briscoe came to know the Lord. She was so excited about her new-found faith that she wanted to tell everyone. So she sent out invitations to a party explaining that she was in love and she would like to introduce her girlfriends to the new man in her life. The date was set and all the party preparations were made. When she explained that she was in love with Jesus, some of her girlfriends were offended and left. Others stood by her. One young lady came to Christ that very night. Have you hosted an "I came to Christ party?"

Some call them "Matthew Parties." Matthew was by trade a tax gatherer. This made him a disrespected pawn of Rome and a traitor to Israel. Because of this, he had few friends beyond the occupation of tax gatherers. Also, because of the hatred of the Jews, he was in danger in the countryside and dared not leave the confines of the city without support and security. One day, while sitting at his tax booth, Jesus came by and uttered two of the most powerful words a person could speak, "Follow me!" Matthew immediately left his booth (and his livelihood) and followed Jesus. Later we see Jesus at the table (Matthew's?) with many tax gatherers and irreligious people there. The Pharisees saw this and questioned why Jesus was "partying" with these unacceptable people. Jesus gave a simple answer. He was there because they were in need of Him. These people understood that they needed Jesus. They were friends of Matthew's, wanted to come to his house, and got to hear from the Master.

Back to the command: In verse 18, Jesus states that He is the ultimate authority over everything in heaven and on earth. It is all- inclusive. There is nothing in heaven and nothing on earth or anything in between, that Jesus is not the master over. Because of that, He is in a position to give a command to His followers. His command is "Go!"

Literally, it is, "as you are going" or "as you find yourself going." It is not an event on the calendar or an item to be checked off your "to do" list. It is a continual mindset that has you obeying the master of the universe every day and everywhere you go.

And as we are going we are to keep in mind five things:

» We are to make disciples. This means followers of Jesus.

» We are to go to all nations and do this. That is a call to foreign missions.

» We are to baptize people in the name of the Father, Son, and the Holy Spirit.

» We are to teach followers of Christ to be obedient.

» We must always keep in mind that we are not alone. Jesus is with us forever and wherever we go.

Since this is a command rather than a suggestion, why is it that we find that so many will not witness to or disciple others? What are the major reasons we hold back from simply obeying? I believe that underneath all the word play and excuse laden comments for disobedience, you will find three major categories to our rebellion against the King's command:

1-Lack of belief. Perhaps we really don't believe that heaven is that good and conversely, that hell is that bad. We read about the glories of heaven and even sing about them. We hear stories of how great heaven is and even come up with our own ideas about what we desire to experience. We express our heartfelt desire to go there and be done with the struggle and heartache this life in our earthen vessel carries. We long for the day that we will no longer see through a "mirror dimly" and want to see Jesus face to face. To have all our questions answered and be reunited with long lost loved ones is our heart's cry.

When my wife agreed to marry me, my heart was filled with so much excitement. It was a most magical evening, second only to the night I accepted Christ. I was so excited that I couldn't wait to tell someone. We drove home from the restaurant and stopped to tell my sister and brother-in-law. We awakened my parents and called her parents. On the way back to our homes in North Carolina, we stopped and told an old friend and asked him to perform our ceremony. I got on the phone and told all my closest friends announcing the fact that we were to be wed in six months. We spent the next six months preparing for that great day. The venue was set. The bridal party was chosen and confirmed. The music was selected. The reception was planned and the invitations were delivered. I remember waking up several times during the night before our wedding day, realizing what day it was, sitting up and raising my hands over my head in silent celebration. When the wedding began, I still remember the moment my eyes caught sight of my lady as she stepped into the aisle. I have no doubt that my heart skipped more than a beat as I thought about this woman saying yes to spend her entire life with me. Even now I am so thrilled to be a part of her life. I am often asked to speak at various gatherings and I always enjoy introducing my wife. Allow me to share with you how I let the audience know something about the woman God gave me;

"This is my wife Pam. She's four-foot-ten on the outside and seven-foot tall on the inside. She loves God, God's word, God's people and the lost. She can out-cook and out-clean any woman this side of the Mississippi. Her Momma's the sweetest woman in North Carolina and she's sweeter than her Momma. And she'll put any man, woman, or child in a headlock who won't admit that Jesus Christ is Lord to the glory of the Father. Now that's my wife!"

The question at hand is not whether or not you love your mate like that. The question is do you love the Lord like that? Is your life with Him worth sharing? Do you really believe that heaven is that great and that a life with God Almighty is worth sharing? Don't we want to go and take as many people with us as possible?

If hell is what the Bible says it is, shouldn't we be doing all we can to keep people out of it? Knowing that hell is a place of eternal separation from God filled with anguish and fear, doesn't that add some motivation to our witnessing and growth plans?

If heaven is what the Bible says it is, what about hell? If hell is what the Bible says it is, shouldn't we be doing all we can to keep people out of it? Knowing that hell is a place of eternal separation from God filled with anguish and fear, doesn't that add some motivation to our witnessing and growth plans? I believe that a glimpse of heaven or a sniff of hell gives urgency to our efforts.

But maybe our reluctantcy is not due to disbelief. Maybe we really do love the Lord and we truly do believe what He says about heaven and hell. What could be our problem then?

2-Lack of love. Perhaps we are so steeped in selfishness that we have become apathetic toward those outside our circle and in particular, those with whom we do not come in contact. Maybe it doesn't bother us that people will miss heaven or experience hell for all eternity. If hell is nearly as bad as the Bible depicts it, we should be screaming to get people's attention and warn them of impending doom.

One of the excuses I hear for not sharing the gospel is, "I don't want to offend people." But how offended will they be when they stand before a holy God and He says to them, "Depart from me, I never knew you." What do you think they will feel toward you if in that moment they are able to look past God's throne and see you on the other side of the gates of heaven enjoying all God has blessed you with. Offended will not even come close to describing what their feelings toward you will be. I would much rather offend people who thank me later when they enter heaven than worry about their feelings toward me now and see them dismissed from the presence of

God later. We need to stop playing games, admit to our lack of love, repent, and get busy.

3-Lack of trust. Three things about Jesus we must be reminded of: He is the creator of the entire universe. He also has ultimate authority over everything. Finally, He promises to be with us wherever we go. Knowing these three things leaves no room for fear or lack of trust. God does not measure success the way we think He does. He is not keeping score by how many people we have won to His kingdom. God is looking for faithfulness. He is looking for a heart that is willing to turn over complete control to Him so that He can work in and through us. All baseball players know if you don't swing, you can't hit a home run. Likewise, in the area of evangelism, if you don't engage in a witnessing opportunity, you will not lead someone to a saving knowledge of Christ. You must push your fear of rejection aside and wade into the waters of a possible eternal life-changing experience.

The key is to gain all the training we can and then launch out into the witnessing opportunities the Lord brings our way.

Some sidestep witnessing because they are deeply afraid that a question will be asked that they don't have an answer for. Obviously, there is always that possibility. A fool can ask more questions than any wise man can answer. But we must not let that deter us. The key is to gain all the training we can and then launch out into the witnessing opportunities the Lord brings our way. We must push back the intimidating possibility that we will look foolish and realize that a person coming to faith in Jesus Christ is more of a process that an event. It most often involves small "sips" of the good news, not a deluge of the gospel.

Perhaps a simplified anatomical example will help. Oxygen enters the bloodstream by chance. The lining of the lungs is made up of strands of tissue that crisscross each other multiple times. Between these strands are microscopic gaps or holes. When a molecule of oxygen enters the lungs by way of inhalation, that molecule *bounces* back and forth numerous times until it hits one of those holes. At that point it *penetrates* the lining and is swept away by the bloodstream. A successful encounter has occurred.

Similarly, when we carry the gospel, we share it with as many people in as many ways as we can. As we engage in witnessing opportunities, we *bounce* from experience to experience and as people encounter more exposure to the good news, they have more opportunities to embrace the Savior.

Alex McFarland knows this. In 2000, he launched a campaign called *50 States in 50 Days-the Tour of Truth*. As the title indicates, the goal was to preach the gospel in 50 states within the course of 50 days. That's a lot of work and organization, and it takes a lot of money and time to do that. But the resultant lives that were changed for all eternity were well worth it.

In Acts 1:8 Jesus tells the disciples, "You shall receive power when the Holy Spirit has come upon you; and you shall be my witnesses both in Jerusalem, and in all Judea and Samaria and even to the remotest part of the earth."

I would propose to you that Jesus is giving us our marching orders. This is not elective material. It is a command. Willingness is not part of the equation. We need to personalize this command and find the areas the Lord is directing us to. For you Jerusalem is your local area. It could be the diner you frequent, the school you attend, your place of employment, or your neighborhood. Judea moves you further from your locale and places you in the state in which you live. Samaria pushes you further out into the mission field in your country. The remotest parts of the earth draw you to foreign missions.

By the way, the early disciples were reluctant to do that, so the Lord brought pressure on them to leave Jerusalem and the protection and comforts of their home turf and caused them to flee into the uttermost parts of the earth. That's how we were able to be exposed to the gospel in the first place.

Acts 8:1 tells us, "…And on that day a great persecution arose against the church in Jerusalem, and they were all scattered throughout the regions of Judea and Samaria except the apostles."

They were running for their lives. They picked up all they could carry and took off leaving the familiar surroundings of Jerusalem and the friends they had there. When they ran far enough and caught their breath, they settled in to telling their story and sharing the relationship they had with Jesus Christ. I'm not implying that God will force you to share, but I am saying that just like the disciples, the Lord will put us in positions so that we can be a witness wherever His hand brings us.

Paul says in I Corinthians 9:22, "I have become all things to all men that I might save some." This means that Paul was willing to get out of his comfort zone and do whatever he needed to because he saw that souls hung in the balance. He was willing to be and do whatever was necessary to lead someone to Jesus. How are you doing with that?

In general, there is a distinct and proper order to the effectiveness of our witnessing. Of course there are exceptions to this, but we must check ourselves in these areas to have maximum impact on those whose paths we cross.

Life

You must portray a lifestyle that backs up rather than contradicts your belief system. Witnessing with your life alone is not enough. Our society abounds with morally upright people. The words must be said, but our lives will always outshout our words.

You must portray a lifestyle that backs up rather than contradicts your belief system.

When Sodom was about to be destroyed, the angels came to Lot and told him to take his family and flee. The city was to be completely destroyed and they were to leave with no time to waste. Lot's daughters were engaged to be married. Naturally Lot wanted to get his future sons-in-law out as well. But because Lot's life ran contrary to his belief in God, they couldn't take him seriously. Genesis 19:14 says, "And Lot went out and spoke to his sons-in-law, who were to marry his daughters, and said, 'Up, get out of this place for the Lord will destroy the city.' But he appeared to his sons-in-law to be jesting."

Because of his life-style and the priorities he demonstrated in his life, even those closest to him couldn't take Lot seriously. He was telling them the Lord was going to destroy their city and everyone in it, but they thought he was just kidding. He couldn't get their attention because he wasn't living what he was selling.

Generally, before people trust Christ, they trust a Christian. And the apex of their trust is centered in how that Christian is living. You have to live it before you give it! They have to see what you really are in order to want what you really have. It is not your circumstances or toys that will drive them to making a commitment to Christ. It is how consistently you handle life and your reactions to what life throws at you. They don't demand that you be perfect in order to win a hearing with them. They just expect you to be genuine. A good place to start is with the fruit the Spirit (Galatians 5:22). When they see love, joy, peace, patience, kindness, goodness, faithfulness, gentleness, and self-control, they will struggle to resist the desire to have what you have. Those around you will be drawn to you like a moth to a flame and you will have the opportunity to share with them what it means to be a follower of Christ.

When people learn of your commitment to Christ, they will constantly be watching you. The true Christian life is life in a fishbowl. There is nowhere to hide.

But you must bear in mind that when people learn of your commitment to Christ, they will constantly be watching you. The true Christian life is life in a fishbowl. There is nowhere to hide. Their motivations for keeping their eye on you may vary. Some will watch you because they are curious about you. Others will be looking for a flaw or mistake in your behavior. Some will ridicule you and try to justify their behavior. Their reasons for observing you are not your concern. You just have to understand that your behavior is constantly on display.

A friend of mine is the pastor of a church. He and his wife had finally gotten to the point where they needed to expand their home. They did everything right in positioning themselves to begin the project. They had gotten all the proper permits, paid all the fees, and lined up all the contractors. Just days before they were to begin, he got a call from his wife who was in tears. Somehow there was a problem with the plans and they were sent a letter telling them that they were not to proceed. My friend was very frustrated and rushed home to grab the plans and head to town hall. He knew they had done everything right. He briskly entered the office, speaking sharply and directly to the woman who attended the desk. He demanded to know what the problem was and didn't hide his emotions. She reached for the plans and said, "let's take a look at these." Then she asked a question that put my friend back a few steps. She asked, "Are these plans for your home or for the church?" At that moment he realized two things: she knew who he was, and he was in no position to talk to her about a relationship with the Lord. I'm not sure whether or not she was a Christian, but I do know that she acted more like one than the preacher did.

The strongest foundation for sharing the gospel is love and the best plans for sharing love is by meeting needs.

Love

Beyond committing to displaying a life worthy of our call, we must have a genuine love for people. That is what will draw them in. Words can be impactful, but there is no better way to communicate love than to meet someone's needs. As you peruse the gospels, you'll find that in virtually every case, Jesus met a person's need before he gave a spiritual truth. The ten lepers were cleansed before they were sent to the priest. The woman caught in adultery was rescued from death before she was told to go and sin no more. Peter experienced the biggest catch of fish before he was told, "follow me." When we meet people's physical needs, we earn the right to address their spiritual needs. Hunger pangs will always outshout any message. We must reach their body before we can reach their hearts.

Oswald Golter was a missionary to China in the mid-1940's. After being on the field for ten years, he was heading home on furlough. While in port in India, he came across some refugees huddled together in a warehouse. He approached them and asked, "What would you like for Christmas?" They looked at him and said, "We're not Christians. We don't believe in Christ." Close by was a bakery displaying German pastries. Golter exchanged his ticket for cash and bought them all a pastry. A man observing this approached Golter and said, "Why did you do that? They don't believe in Christ." He simply responded, "I know. But I do." The strongest foundation for sharing the gospel is love and the best plans for sharing love is by meeting needs.

Lips

It's not enough to live a life that is consistent morally. It's not enough to be motivated to help people by love. We cannot escape the fact that sooner or later we must share the words that will kindle their hearts and cause them to embrace the Savior. Verbally sharing the good news of Jesus Christ need not be complex or nerve wracking. If you have had a genuine conversion to Jesus Christ and you know John 3:16, you have the foundation you need to lead others to Christ. Now all you need is the opportunity and the courage.

Tell them where you were on your journey to Jesus. Be careful not to give too many details about how the devil was running the show. This is about a relationship with Christ, not Satan. Tell how you made a commitment to the Lord and share what a difference it has made in your life. There are a multitude of verses you could point someone to, but if you center on John 3:16, you will be able to tell them:

1. God loves you.

2. Christ came to be the sacrifice for all the times we messed up. We just need to ask Him to forgive us.

3. Sincerely believing and trusting in Christ is all that is neces-

sary for a person to experience eternal forgiveness and ensure a place in heaven.

I fully realize that this is highly simplistic, but I also understand that most of the requirements we share with people don't come from the Holy Scriptures. They come from our ideas regarding salvation. It really is much simpler than we make it out to be.

So many of us know that we are to speak the truth in love as Ephesians 4:15 says. But too often we are long on truth and short on love. I have often paused when I've heard street preachers screaming at all those who pass by and I wonder where is the love. If they do convert anyone (and I have yet to meet someone converted by a screaming preacher), I'm sure they could be labeled a *bloody convert.* I commend these preachers for their zeal but question their techniques. Personally, I have led many people to Christ, but I've never *yelled* one into glory.

There are some particular keys that will put us in a position to lead others to Christ:

A- Be Prepared-The Bible tells us that we must be prepared "in season and out of season" to preach the word (Ephesians 4:15). I Peter 3:15 tells us, "…but sanctify Christ as Lord in your hearts, always being ready to make a defense to everyone who asks you to give an account for the hope that is in you, yet with gentleness and reverence."

While serving at a week-long Christian camp, my wife had forgotten something in our room. A while later she came back beaming and explained that she had just led the cleaning lady to trust in Jesus Christ. This happened because she was prepared in season and out, and she spoke to this woman in truth and love. She didn't need to tell the woman to wait while she got her husband. She took the Scriptures that she had in her head and shared them with a woman who decided to trust in Christ.

B-Study-The Christian life is the best life, but it's not an easy life. There are no such things as *sanctification pills.* When you come to Christ, you are expected to be about your Heavenly Father's business.

II Timothy 2:15 tells us, "Be diligent to present yourself approved to God as a workman who does not need to be ashamed, accurately handling the word of truth." Basically, we are expected to grow in Christ and in the knowledge of the truth. Just as we would expect a child to grow and mature into an adult, we expect babes in Christ to grow into mature followers.

C-Use Your Assets-In a short exercise you will be able to come up with a sizable list of your abilities and gifts at your disposal. These assets fall into two distinct camps. Some are intangible. Perhaps you hold a particular position of authority, or you can sing, speak, write, encourage, show hospitality, teach, or have an ample amount of free time. Some assets are tangible. These are those involving money, tools, equipment, space or even recreational toys. Whatever it is that you have access to, the key is to find creative ways to use it to share the gospel with those the Lord puts in your life.

I've learned of an optometrist who has rewritten the words that his patients would read as he checks their vision. The standard sentence is, "Now is the time for all good men to come to the aid of their country." However, when a patient looks into his machine, he finds the words, "God loves you and has a wonderful plan for your life." That is a creative use of assets.

While serving on a university campus as a teacher and athletic trainer, I would constantly invite the student/athletes to a Christian meeting. One particular football player named Jamie always said he would come but never showed up. Something always seemed to come up keeping him away. One day after practice I told him, "Hey Jamie! You gotta come to the meeting tonight. We have a very special guest and if you show up, I'll introduce you." He wanted to know who it was, but I refused to tell him and just reiterated that if he showed up, I'd introduce him. He did show up and came right up to me and said, "Okay, I'm here. Now who's the special guest?" I said, "You are!" and then I spent the next several minutes introducing him to the others. I fully admit that was a little deceptive, but he had no trouble forgiving me when he found a new life in Christ.

Billy Graham came to Christ by way of Albert McMachan who let him drive his truck. A truck motivated Billy Graham to hear Mordeccai Hamm who led him to Christ.

During a snowstorm, fifteen-year-old C.H. Spurgeon came to a primitive Methodist church and entered to get out of the weather. The weather kept the preacher away so a member of the congregation without any training got up and spoke from the text. Spurgeon came to Christ that day. An untrained believer preached C.H. Spurgeon into being a follower of Christ.

By reading Martin Luther's preface to the book of Romans (not even the full text) John Wesley came to salvation. An introduction to a text caused John Wesley to commit his life to Jesus.

I was at a Fellowship of Christian Athletes camp where a young man quipped, "I came to see my gods. But then I heard about their God. And in the end, their God became my God." The natural platform of athletics caused a young man to accept the Lord as his Saviour. You too have assets. You just have to figure out how to use them to introduce someone to Christ.

D-Pray for Opportunities. It may very well be that God is arranging your life and the life of someone else in order to have them intersect one another. We need to pray for open eyes. The look on someone's face, a comment made, a circumstance observed, can all be clues that someone is in a position to listen to you tell about the Savior. A person's heart will lead you to the need. Pray for those opportunities, keep your head on a swivel, and keep your heart attuned to the Holy Spirit.

The look on someone's face, a comment made, a circumstance observed, can all be clues that someone is in a position to listen to you tell about the Savior. A person's heart will lead you to the need.

E-Do what you enjoy doing and invite someone to join you. What is it that you do for fun? Camping, hiking, movies, dining, cooking, car shows, shopping, concerts are all avenues to invite someone to spend time with you. Keep in mind the adage, *no contact-no impact.* You must arrange for and commit to time spent with non-Christians if you are going to have an opportunity to share His story.

A friend of mine enjoys going to the movies. Because of that he started a ministry in his church called *reel evangelism.* He invites three other Christian couples to join him and targets another couple he believes does not know Christ. They go to dinner and then the theatre. After the show, they meet at someone's house for dessert and discuss the movie. By design, the conversation always turns to spiritual issues and a bridge is built toward sharing the gospel.

A little boy attended Sunday school for the first time. Upon returning home his mother asked him, "Who was your teacher?" He replied, "Jesus' Grandmother." Peaking her interest she asked him, "How do you know she was Jesus' Grandmother?" The boy simply said, "Because that's all she talked about the whole time."

This brings us to this question: Who is it that you are talking about all the time? There can be no doubt. You can be a witness!

SHARING PIECES:

Have you ever led someone to a salvation decision? If so, what happened?

Share a creative way to witness.

What is the strongest roadblock you see to sharing your faith?

Give five key points that you feel any witness should have.

PRINCIPLE #8
YOU CAN BE A MENTOR

"WE MUST BE CAREFUL OF THAT CRITICAL MOMENT WHEN AN OLD HAND REACHES FORWARD AND A YOUNG HAND REACHES BACK STRAINING FOR THE BATON." -UNKNOWN

In Homer's *Odyssey,* Odysseus is preparing to leave to fight in the Trojan war. His son Telemachus is to be left behind with his mother Athena. Before leaving, Odysseus charges his friend to look after his son and keep him safe. He is also to impart to him wisdom and knowledge. The name of Odysseus' friend is Mentor and therein lies the origin of the position one takes today in the task of imparting wisdom and knowledge to one who is less experienced.

The idea of mentoring someone strikes fear in so many people's hearts. But the command to mentor must not be overlooked. Previously we covered the idea of The *great commission.* This brought us to the command to lead others to follow Christ. But the other part of the command has to do with maturing someone who has made a decision to follow the Lord. After the *born again* event takes place in their lives we are expected to help the person grow into maturity. The other part of the great commission states, "…make disciples of all the nations….teaching them to observe all that I commanded you." (Matthew 28:19-20).

The Bible is replete with examples of the mentor/student relationship. Abraham looked after his nephew Lot. Eli raised Samuel. Elijah taught Elisha. Paul mentored Timothy and Barnabus took John Mark under his wing. Each of these examples and many more demonstrate the mentoring process. Each of them carried the elements of discipleship and teaching.

I have always had someone in my life that filled the role of the mentor both formally and informally. In high school a man named Howard led our youth group and taught me (mostly by example) how to walk as a Christian young man. He talked me into going on a Bible quiz show and coached me through it (I did terribly but had my moment of fame). He arranged for me to be trained to lead backyard five-day clubs. He and his wife picked me up so I could go to the Easter sunrise service at the mall. He led us on hikes and trips to the beach and Bible studies.

In college, I met regularly with Don, the pastor of the church I attended. He talked with me about the Scriptures and about life on campus. He also helped me understand the importance of living out my faith. Gareth "Lefty" Biser was not only my faculty advisor, but he was like a father to me while I was away from home. Because he was the athletic trainer he took care of me physically, but he did so much more in looking after my soul. During the summers I met with a man named John. We would meet for coffee or dessert and cover a wide range of topics from history, to Bible, to mechanics. He poured into my life more encouragement than he will ever realize. Even today, I have a friend named Stephen, an older minister who always shares great advice and is a plethora of information. His knowledge of the Bible and history always leads us into such great conversations, and I wouldn't trade the hours we've spent together for anything. Having a mentor is essential if you're going to grow to become all the Lord wants you to be. Being a mentor is just as vital.

So much emphasis is placed on the benefits the student receives that it is easy to miss all the benefits the mentor gets. As a result of pouring oneself into someone else's life, you'll gain great joy and satisfaction as you help the person grow into a more mature Christian. You'll find yourself studying, planning, and thinking more about your own walk with Christ and you'll grow in the process. Too many who name the name of Christ are satisfied with sitting on the sidelines and watching the game. They go to church and perhaps read their Bibles, but when it comes to being a game changer they are satisfied with letting someone else fill that role. They attend church and sit and soak. There is nothing wrong with coming to church and being filled with wisdom from God's word. But there has to be a purpose behind it. If you sit and soak long enough, you will sour. That's when you look around you and see all the things you're not happy with, and you spend your time complaining. We are expected to sit and soak but only to the point where we are equipped to serve.

In the northern part of Israel lies the Sea of Galilee. It's about twelve miles long and seven miles wide and is lush and green and teeming with life. Cities and towns are in abundance around this body of water. Tourism, crop irrigation, and the fishing industry thrive there. Flowing out of the Sea of Galilee is the Jordan River. Approximately fifty miles due south is the Dead Sea. In contrast, it is about forty-one miles long, and eleven miles wide. It is the lowest body of water on earth being about four hundred meters below sea level. Because of this it boasts the highest concentration of salt of any body of water on the planet. Due to this high concentration, nothing grows in the Dead Sea--no fish, or plants, not even bacteria, hence the name *Dead Sea*. But what is the cause of the difference between these two bodies of water? The reason the Sea of Galilee is so full of life and the Dead Sea so void of it is simply due to its connecting sources. The Sea of Galilee is fed by underground streams and the Jordan River which runs through it from the north to the south. Conversely, the Dead Sea receives its water from the Jordan River but because it is so far below sea level, it has no out-port. Whatever it takes in it keeps.

If we do nothing but consume, we'll become swollen, full, and dead.

So it is in our lives if we are only a "receiving vessel." If we do nothing but consume, we'll become swollen, full, and dead. Like the Sea of Galilee, we must have an *out-port* if we are to remain vibrant and full of life. That is the recipe for growth. That is a picture of the mentoring process. Like breathing, you must take in air and dispel air to sustain your life. In mentoring, you take in knowledge and then you impart knowledge to someone else. But what is necessary in the mentoring process?

1. You must be more mature than the one you are mentoring. You cannot lead from the back. It is the difference between pushing a string and pulling a string. You don't necessarily have to be older than the one you are leading although that will be the case most often, but you must be more mature in your walk with the Lord. You will find that you lead out of your abundance and you can take your student no farther than you have gone yourself. That is where study comes in. You must be a student of the word and be able to impart that word to the one you'll be spending time with.

2. Your time must be centered on the Bible. Because we are commanded to make disciples not buddies, (although you will find yourself becoming good friends), you must be intentional about spiritual growth. Small talk is fine but when you plan time together, you must get past talk of sports, money, decorating tips, and politics. You have to decide how you will spend your time. Will they come away knowing more about themselves and their Lord, or will they come away just knowing more about things that carry little or no eternal value?

3. You must have a plan. There must be some organizational idea in mind as you begin spending time together. It's not just a matter of being friends, it's beyond that. You are expected to grow them up in the Lord. You might plan on studying a particular book or character from the Bible. Maybe a specific book by a well-known author is the direction you'll take. Perhaps an individual topic (i.e. money, marriage, leadership) is where you want to focus your time.

4. It must be practical. It's fine and even fun to talk on the theoretical level. But sooner or later you have to get past the *what?* and deal with the *so what?* That's where the proverbial rubber meets the road. You have to ask yourself, "what do I want them to know? and…what do I want them to do?" That's when *talking* transitions to *walking*. When studying a particular passage of Scripture there are four key questions that must be traversed:

What does it say? This is the literal meaning of the text. This is where you study individual words and phrases and look for cross-references.

What does it mean? Here, you put the passage in today's language. You might explain John 3:16 as saying, God loves you so much, in fact, He loves the world so much that He was willing to send His Son Jesus Christ to die for us all so that if we put our faith and trust in

Him, we would not experience eternal death but would have eternal life.

How is it illustrated? We learn by hearing, but we remember by illustration. That was Jesus' most common method of teaching. He told a truth and then told a story. This is commonly called a parable, and it is simply a story designed to drive home a point. When illustrating part of John 3:16, I often use the illustration of the *whosoever door*. If you have ever seen a dog in the aisle of a grocery store, then you will be able to relate to the concept of the *whosoever door*. The automatic door to the super market has a beam that opens the door whenever the beam is crossed. The door doesn't care what crosses the beam. It could be a man, woman, child, or a dog. The beam is non-discriminatory. The size, shape, color, or character of the object crossing the beam doesn't matter. When the beam is crossed, the door opens. That is the *whosoever door*. And God's *whosoever door* is Jesus Christ and the cross. Whosoever believes in Him and the sacrificial work He did on the cross will have the door to eternity opened to him.

How is it applied? Now that they know, what will they do? It's not enough to have knowledge imparted to the head and even the heart. We must put *shoe leather* to the knowledge we have. In the book of living quotations we find these words, "If it doesn't affect your hands and feet, it isn't Christianity." This is where challenges come in. When they have a good grasp on what you're covering, you must get them to the point where they can demonstrate it in their lives.

"If it doesn't affect your hands and feet, it isn't Christianity." -Book of Living Quotations

While working on the university campus, two colleagues and I formed a Bible study. We were covering a passage of Scripture in James 1:22, "But prove yourselves doers of the word, and not merely hearers who delude themselves." In this Bible verse we are directed to go beyond just studying the word, but to putting it into practice in a literal sense. So we decided to challenge each other. We came up with the idea that each of us would share a Bible directive with the other two and that person would have to live those verses out during the following week and report back to the group. The verses I selected were fairly clear and easy to put into practice, something along the lines of loving your neighbor as yourself and honoring your father and mother.

One of the two that I received was a good bit more challenging and it took a lot more effort on my part. I got a verse in Luke 6. Verse 12 says, "It was at this time that He went off to the mountain to pray, and He spent the whole night in prayer to God." There's not a lot of wiggle room in that verse. Jesus went to the mountain. Jesus prayed. Jesus spent the entire night in prayer. The application is clear. When the weekend came, I put my verse into action. I knew I couldn't stay awake if I remained in one place so I got out my hat and coat, grabbed a flashlight, and headed down the street. I walked and prayed all night. I prayed about everything and anything. I prayed for old friends and people I've never met. I covered politicians and performers. I sat on the steps of a church and prayed for the pastor and people. I prayed over homes and families as I walked passed. By morning light, I traveled a long way both on foot and in prayer. That's application!

5. You both must be committed to the process. If only one of you is on board with the process of spiritual mentoring, it will not work. If two people are in a boat and each given an oar, but only one person rows, not only will you go downstream but you'll do it while making circles. It may be difficult to be consistent. Life can throw us some curve balls, and there's always the possibility of something unplanned coming up. But you must do your best to commit to the process and meet regularly.

I mentored a young man for several years. We generally would meet on the same day of the week at a particular restaurant. We got to know the workers, the menu, and each other very well. Those were very rich times of study, discussion, and growth. Without a dual commitment, the process moving forward is very difficult if not impossible.

6. You must set goals. You have to know what you want to accomplish and how long you anticipate it taking to reach those goals. Someone has rightly said, "A goal is a dream with a deadline." So you can decide that you will cover one chapter in a particular book each week or plan on five sessions on a specific topic. But you should be able to make statements like, "By the end of this year or month, we will cover this book having discussed each chapter including ways we can put it to use." Perhaps you can set a goal of memorizing fifty Bible verses in one year. You might come up with an outline of twenty-five essential spiritual truths you need to teach your kids. Whatever your goals may be, you'll find that you will cover more ground and grow deeper in your walk with the Lord as you bring someone along on the journey. You can be a spiritual mentor!

SHARING PIECES:

Have you ever mentored anyone or been mentored by someone? If so, share what that was like.

____

____

____

____

What five key truths would you share with someone you are mentoring?

____

____

____

____

What is one thing you feel mentoring would cost you? Share why you would be reluctant to pay it.

____

____

____

____

PRINCIPLE # 9
YOU CAN HAVE A MINISTRY

"YOU CAN NEVER DO A KINDNESS TOO SOON FOR YOU NEVER KNOW HOW SOON IT WILL BE TOO LATE." -RALPH WALDO EMERSON

Too many people come to the erroneous conclusion that they must learn more, experience more, or get a degree in order to develop a ministry. They trudge their way through the Christian life with a deep sense of inadequacy and live their lives with the idea that eventually they will be ready to take on a particular ministry and make a difference for the Kingdom of God. They have concluded that they either don't have the skills necessary to be successful or that their past mistakes have disqualified them from service. Here's a news flash- *TODAY IS YOUR DAY TO DISCOVER YOUR MINISTRY AND START MAKING A DIFFERENCE IN PEOPLE'S LIVES!*

Following is a confidential report on several candidates being considered for ministry:

Adam: Good man, but problems with his wife. Also one reference told of how he and his wife enjoy walking naked in the woods.

Noah: Former pastorate of 120 years with not even one convert. Prone to unrealistic building projects.

David: The most promising leader of all until we discovered the affair he had with his neighbor's wife and the scandal that followed in an effort to cover it up.

Elisha: Reported to have lived with a single widow while at his former church. Given to deep moments of discouragement even after great success.

John: Says he is a Baptist, but definitely doesn't dress like one. Has slept in the outdoors for months on end, has a weird diet, and provokes denominational leaders.

Peter: Too blue collar. Has a bad temper (even been known to curse). Had a big run-in with Paul in Antioch. Aggressive, but a loose cannon.

Paul: Powerful CEO type leader and fascinating preacher. However, short on tact, unforgiving with younger ministers, harsh, and has been known to preach all night.

Timothy: Too young!

Methuselah: Too old…Way too old!

Jesus: Has had popular times, but once his church grew to 5,000 he managed to offend them all, and then this church dwindled down to twelve people. Seldom stays in one place very long, and of course, he's single.

Judas: His references are solid. A steady plodder. Conservative. Good connections. Knows how to handle money. Strong possibilities here.

You'll have to go a long way before you can find the perfect candidate. On paper all people look different than they really are. This should give you hope as you meander around to find your ministry.

Hebrews 10:23-25 reminds us, "Let us hold fast the confession of our hope without wavering, for He who promised is faithful; and let us consider how to stimulate one another to love and good deeds, not forsaking our own assembling together, as is the habit of some, but encouraging one another; and all the more as you see the day drawing near."

There are three basic directives in this scripture reference: We are to hold on to our faith without any compromise. We are to come up with ways we can motivate each other to be busy in the Lord's work. We are to be a point of encouragement to each other. That is the essence of ministry. We minister as an extension of our faith. We find ways to use the gifts we have. We encourage each other in the use of our individual and collective gifts. When we engage in these points of ministry, we will find that we have something to believe in, something to do with our belief, and someone with whom we can live out our belief.

There are two distinct categories of ministry: ministry to the body of believers and ministry to those who are lost.

Every believer is called to minister and every ministry has some element of giving help to someone else. There are two distinct categories of ministry: ministry to the body of believers and ministry to those who are lost. The difference between the two is that when you minister to the lost, you are gaining the right to share the gospel. When you minister to the saved, you gain the right to call them brother or sister. Meeting a need of the saved makes their lives better. Meeting a need of the lost makes their eternal life possible.

There are two main categories of ministry:

1-Verbal ministry. This is a ministry whereby a person is helped through the various means of communication. Words have tremendous power. They can bring you up on your worst day or tear you down from the pinnacle of success. While driving recently, I received a call from a member of our church who needed some information. I gave it to him and hung up. Moments later he called again. He simply said, "I forgot to tell you, my wife and I really love you!" What an encouraging message. Beyond just the words was the message that he went out of his way to convey.

2-Tangible ministry. This is a ministry where you are actually doing something for someone. It's mowing the lawn, delivering a meal, building a house, baking a cake, helping someone move, or anything else that simply employs physical labor.

Beyond these categories of ministry are three sub-areas of ministry:

Social ministry-this is ministry that seeks to make people feel at home and welcome. When a neighbor brings over some cookies to a family that just moved in, that is a social ministry. Sitting with someone, welcoming a person into a group, or inviting a couple to a party are all examples of social ministry.

Physical ministry is doing anything physical for someone. When you help fix a car, clean a house, or watch pets, you are performing a physical ministry.

Spiritual ministry is any ministry that enables a person to grow spiritually. When you mentor, encourage, pray with, or explain scriptures to someone, you are performing a spiritual ministry. And when you employ your spiritual gift, you find deep and satisfying fulfillment.

Our motivation for ministry should start and end with love. The Bible tells us, "love covers a multitude of sins" (I Peter 4:8b). What that means is my love for you will help me overlook any overt flaw you may have in your personality or behavior. You don't have to look, talk, or behave exactly as I do. Because I love you, I can bring myself to forgive you for anything that brings you into conflict with me. Conversely, because you love me, you will be able to look past my faults and struggles as well. Love allows us to do that for one another. I Corinthians 13:4-7 says, "Love is patient, love is kind, and is not jealous; love does not brag and is not arrogant, does not act unbecomingly; it does not seek its own, is not provoked, does not take into account a wrong suffered, does not rejoice in unrighteousness but rejoices with the truth; bears all things, believes all things, hopes all things, endures all things." Admittedly, some people are easier to love than others. Personality conflicts exist even within the body of Christ. It reminds me of the old ditty,

> "To live above with the saints we love, ah, that is the purest glory! To live below with the saints we know, ah, that's a another story."

Love for each other is a mark of discipleship. It is our calling card that distinguishes us from those who don't follow Christ. John 13:35 tells us, "By this all men will know that you are My disciples, if you have love for one another." This type of love leads naturally to obedience and service. There are a plethora of inventories and surveys that will indicate what a person's spiritual gifts are, but for the most part they have their roots in I Corinthians 12. The various gifts the body of Christ has been given are outlined here. These gifts are given to us in various measures for the building up of the body of Christ and the glory of God. We get the benefits and He gets the glory. As with any gift, there is an inherent danger in its employment. Following is a list and explanation of the different gifts available to the believer along with the subsequent danger through misuse or abuse of each gift.

Administration. This is the ability to organize and coordinate people and tasks. The danger lies in the possibility of losing flexibility and developing a *my way or no way* attitude.

Evangelism. A person with this gift has a heart for the lost and a desire to lead others to witnessing. However, there is a tendency to push all programs and people to evangelism to the exclusion of other areas of ministry.

Exhortation. These are the encouragers. They are naturally attracted to others who want to grow in their walk with Christ and are great catalysts for maturing Christians. But they can be overbearing and impatient with those who don't move as fast as they determine they should.

Giving. People with the gift of giving see real joy in sharing and are constantly looking for needs they can meet. The caution here is that they tend to believe every story they hear and can lack discernment regarding where real needs are.

Helps. These followers of Christ want to help others in their ministry, especially leaders. They go out of their way to help others be more effective. However, many times, while helping others they neglect their families and sometimes themselves.

Hospitality. This is very similar to helps. They have a desire to make others feel at home and welcome. They enjoy both attending parties as well as hosting. The danger here is that often they become over anxious over details and how others feel.

Leadership. This has to do with the ability to take charge and lead others in a particular task or goal. Those with this gift are visionary and goal oriented. However, many times they miss details in looking at the big picture. They also tend to disregard others' feelings in their pursuit of completing the task.

Mercy. Those with the gift of mercy sense immediate compassion for others who are suffering physically, emotionally, or spiritually. They are quickly drawn to those in distress. The downside of this gift is that they tend to carry other's burdens with them and may have difficulty letting them go.

Prophesy. Prophets proclaim God's word without compromise. They have strong convictions and expect others to have that same level of conviction. But they usually live in a black and white world and can be harsh toward others.

Service. People with this gift have a deep desire to meet practical needs. They are quick to volunteer to take up a task and perform their jobs with joy. The danger here is one of self-inflicted injury in that they really struggle with saying *No* and they can wear themselves out easily.

Shepherding. Shepherds take responsibility for the long-term spiritual growth of an individual or group of believers. They are motivated by those in their charge and enjoy gently leading them along. But in doing so they often get discouraged by the group's (or individual's) lack of motivation, progress, or commitment.

Teaching. This is the ability to explain God's truth to others so they can understand it and apply it. However teachers tend to see everything as a platform for a lesson causing others to lose patience with them.

Making a cursory examination of the life of Christ, you will see each of these gifts exemplified.

Administration-He sent them out in two's. (Luke 10:1)

Evangelism-"Go therefore and make disciples…" (Matthew 28:19)

Exhortation-"Seek first His kingdom and His righteousness and all these things shall be added to you." (Matthew 6:33)

Giving-"The Son of Man did not come to be served, but to serve, and to give His life a ransom for many." (Matthew 20:28)

Helps- "Cast the net on the right-hand side of the boat, and you will find a catch." (John 21:6)

Hospitality-"Follow me, and I will make you fishers of men." (Matthew 4:19)

Leadership-"If I want him to remain until I come what is that to you? You follow me!" (John 21:22)

Mercy-"Father, forgive them; for they do not know what they are doing." (Luke 23:34)

Prophesy-"You hypocrites! Rightly did Isaiah prophesy of you…" (Matthew 15:7)

Service-"…rose from supper, and laid aside His garments; and taking a towel He girded Himself about. Then He poured water into the basin and began to wash the disciples' feet, and to wipe them with the towel with which He was girded." (John 13:4-5)

Shepherding-"And He appointed twelve, that they might be with Him and that He might send them out to preach." (Mark 3:14)

Teaching-"And He was teaching them many things in parables." (Mark 4:2)

It is vital that you find your area of ministry. Bear in mind that recognizing a need is not the same as a call. Just because there is a need and you have the time to meet that ministry need does not mean you are the one to do it. If you volunteer to serve in an area you are not gifted in, three things will happen: You will be frustrated. You will frustrate those around you. The quality of your work will fall short of excellent. You must strive to be a *round peg in a round hole.*

Recognizing a need is not the same as a call. Just because there is a need and you have the time to meet that ministry need does not mean you are the one to do it.

Years ago, while serving in a small church and attending seminary, a minister friend of mine stopped to fill his tank before heading off to school. The man at the gas station was a member of the church where my friend was serving. His car was filled up, but when he went to pay the man, his money was refused. The man said, "I can't preach, teach, or sing, but I can pump gas. And if you'll come by here each week, I'll fill your tank for free." My friend was overwhelmed by this kindness. And for three years he never paid for his gas when filling up at that station. The man at the station was exercising his gift of helps.

I have personally noticed that the happiest and most fulfilled Christians are those who have discovered their spiritual gift and enthusiastically used it in creative ways. I've seen meals cooked, patients visited, classes taught, money given, encouragement offered, lawns mowed, children mentored, and cars repaired.

I watched in admiration as a member of our congregation sat up all night with an elderly man who lost his wife earlier that day. I witnessed a couple that came up with the idea of a sports ministry in our church. I saw a man give money secretly to buy Bibles for a group of kids. I noticed a woman sitting with another woman praying and giving her counsel regarding a marriage that was failing. I know a family that took in another family when their house was foreclosed on. I've seen a man take ownership of a men's ministry and lead it to become the biggest and most active in our association. I know a man in our church who forgave a large and legitimate debt owed to him acknowledging that God was able to make it up to him. These—and so many more examples of followers of Christ availing themselves of the power of the Holy Spirit to direct them in ways to serve people and please the Master. Jesus said, "Inasmuch as you have done it to the least of these my brethren, you have done it unto me." (Matthew 25:40).

Martin of Tours is noted as the first military chaplain. He served the Roman army and gave aid to soldiers and others where they battled. On a cold winter day he came across a beggar at the city gate. He had no money, no food, and no place to offer him to stay. All he had was the battered old cloak on his back. He took it off and cut it in half giving half to the beggar. That night, he had a dream. He saw Jesus surrounded by angels. He noticed that Jesus was wearing the cloak he had given the beggar. The angels asked the Master, "Where did you get that dirty old cloak?" With a hint of a smile, Jesus responded, "My servant Martin gave it to me."

And so it is as you and I discover the gifts we've been given and determine to use them to serve those the Heavenly Father loves and deems worthy to die for. Christ considers it a gift that we have given to Him!

You can have a ministry!

SHARING PIECES:

What would you say is your spiritual gift? How have you employed it?

If you knew you couldn't fail, what ministry would you most like to lead or be involved in?

What is the most enjoyable aspect of ministry for you?

PRINCIPLE # 10
YOU CAN GROW

"PRAISE GOD FOR THE HAMMER, THE FILE, AND THE FURNACE." -SAMUEL RUTHERFORD

I enjoy watching the nature channel. The wonders of the creation never cease to amaze me and they continue to give evidence of the great hand of God. Recently I watched a show on sharks. It was fascinating! I learned about the great sense of smell they possess and that each time a great white shark bites down on its prey, it closes its eyes for protection. But I also learned two amazing facts about sharks. I found out that sharks do not have the ability to swim backwards. In fact, if you were to drag a shark backwards through the water, it would suffocate. They are created to always move forward. I also learned that a shark will not outgrow its environment. If you take a young shark and put it in a tank it will grow no larger than what is comfortable. The show displayed a fully mature shark that was six inches long.

As I watched that show, it occurred to me that a lot of Christians are struggling with one or both of those situations. They are suffocating because the world keeps pulling them backward, and they are not growing because they are not in an environment that will foster or even allow their growth.

A friend of mine was interviewing for a position as a pastor in a church. During the interview he was asked to explain his background. He told them several things and ended his answer with the words, "then I completed my education in 1979 at divinity school." After the interview, one of the older members of the panel gently pulled him aside and said, "Son, I hope you don't ever complete your education. Be a life-long learner."

The Bible speaks to that. In Ephesians 4:11-16 we read, "And he gave some as apostles, and some as prophets, and some as evangelists, and some as pastors and teachers for the equipping of the saints for the work of service, to the building up of the body of Christ; until we all attain to the unity of the faith, and of the knowledge of the Son of God, to a mature man, to the measure of the stature which belongs to the fullness of Christ. As a result, we are no longer to be children, tossed here and there by waves, and carried about by every wind of doctrine, by the trickery of men, by craftiness in deceitful scheming; but speaking the truth in love, we are to grow up in all aspects into Him, who is the head, even Christ from whom the whole body, being fitted and held together by that which every joint supplies, according to the proper working of each individual part, causes the growth of the body for the building up of itself in love."

Your chronological age does not necessarily indicate your spiritual age. It is quite possible that a person who has been walking with the Lord for twenty years may not be as spiritually mature as someone who has been saved for five years.

In essence, this passage of Scripture is about growing up—maturing in the faith. It needs to be understood that growing old does not mean growing up. We somehow believe that just because someone has been walking with the Lord for a number of years that this person must be mature. That is not always the case. Your chronological age does not necessarily indicate your spiritual age. It is quite possible that a person who has been walking with the Lord for twenty years may not be as spiritually mature as someone who has been saved for five years. It all depends on what is done to bring about the maturing process.

The above passage speaks about gifts being given for a purpose—to build up those around us. It speaks of the idea of maturing beyond the ways of a child who is tossed about by every idea and scheme that comes down the pike. It describes a person who is spiritually mature enough to recognize the truth from error. And when maturity comes to the entire body of believers, the entire body is lifted up to a new level of growth and understanding. This is growth that is not only possible but is expected.

Just as one would expect a child to grow up and drop his childish ways and attitudes, so God expects His children to grow up and leave behind childish things. In I Corinthians 13:11, Paul tells us, "When I was a child, I used to speak as a child, think as a child, reason as a child; when I became a man, I did away with childish things." Paul is saying that he grew up and no longer speaks, thinks, or reasons like a child. He is chiding us to grow up as well.

There is no getting around it. If you want to be productive for the Kingdom of God, you must have a depth about you that puts you in a position to make a difference. This comes from a deep personal walk with the Lord, a committed prayer life, an intentional avenue of service, and an integrated knowledge of the Bible. Without all of these, your personal growth will be truncated. No roots, no shoots, no fruits!

A few years ago, I spoke with Elmer Towns. He was known as *Mr. Sunday School.* He had been speaking, writing, and encouraging followers of Christ to go deeper in their walk with the Lord and to equip others to do the same. At the time he was eighty-years old and had been on the move for decades. He spoke realistically about having to adjust his ministry due to his age. He never once mentioned quitting or sitting on the sidelines and watching the parade go by. He said his goal now was to "Write everything I know and teach everything I've written." That's a description of a man who has grown up and matured to gigantic proportions.

As we've seen in Ephesians 4:13-16, Paul wanted the Ephesian church to grow up. "As a result, we are no longer to be children, tossed here and there by waves, and carried about by every wind of doctrine, by the trickery of men, by craftiness in deceitful scheming; but speaking the truth in love we are to grow up in all aspects into Him, who is the head, even Christ, from whom the whole body, being fitted and held together by that which every joint supplies, according to the proper working of each individual part, causes the growth of the body for the building up of itself in love." Certain key words jump from the page regarding maturation:

V. 13, *Mature Man.*

V. 14, *No Longer Children.*

V. 15, *Grow Up.*

V. 16, *Growth Of The Body.*

We are not to be children in our theology or actions. We should grow to the point where we are able to defend the faith and deal with some of the deeper issues of Christianity. I have nothing against singing children's songs, but somehow our depth of understanding must get beyond *Jesus Loves Me, This I Know* and *The B-I-B-L-E.* That is foundational to our faith but deep inside we know there's more to it than that.

I am highly frustrated by those who only get what you give them. They grow because they are spoon fed bits of the gospel and sips of theology. They never dig for themselves and cull through the Scriptures to see what God has for them. I cringe when someone hands me a CD of a sermon recently heard. I know the motivation is to help me grow, but I want to be careful not to preach what God gave another man. It has nothing to do with me not feeling that I can glean truth from others. It's just that I want to go to the Lord to see what He has for me personally. We see in Exodus 34:29 that when Moses came down from the mountain after being with the Lord, his face glowed. He didn't even know it but the people couldn't help but see the shining face of the man of God because he had been in the presence of God. Notice also, that nowhere in the text does it say that the peoples' faces glowed because they were with Moses. I want my face to glow as a result of being personally involved with God and entering into His presence on my own. I don't want *ricochet radiance.* I want to grow and glow as a result of digging deeper into the heart of the word of God.

In the Indian culture there is a particular curse that is bestowed on others in moments of anger. It simply says, "May you always remain in one place." That means the desire is for the other person never to travel, never to experience new things, never to grow. But we as

Christians are admonished to grow up in the Lord. Our prime example is Jesus Himself. Luke 2:52, tells us, "Jesus kept increasing in wisdom and stature and in favor with God and men."

This outlines for us four primary areas we are expected to grow in if we are to grow like Jesus. Jesus grew in wisdom. That is the intellectual area of our lives. Jesus also grew in stature. That is the physical side of our lives. He grew in favor with God. That is how He grew spiritually. He also grew in favor with man. That is the social side of life. How are you doing in these four areas? Are you stretching yourself to be like Jesus and grow in all four categories?

No one can grow for you. You must do it yourself. Real growth is intentional, not accidental. You must come up with a plan that will help you grow in all the areas mentioned above. Beyond that, you must submit to the process of growth in the plan you develop. Perhaps you want to lose weight, take a class, travel, or read your Bible through in a year. Each of these requires a plan and a commitment and each of these is unrelated to your age. You can grow no matter where you are in your journey or how far you have come.

You were meant to grow and become more than you are. Ask Him for strength and motivation. Ask Him for direction. Ask Him for companions.

My friend retired from working as a manager in a factory. One day he came up to me very excited. He explained how he bought some woodworking equipment and was now learning how to use it. He told me all about the projects he was working on and how he had organized his shop. He noted that his new hobby gave him a new lease on life. He was having fun. He was learning. He was trying new things. He was growing even after retirement age.

Eagles are fascinating birds. They grow to massive sizes, possess amazing eyesight, and can glide for miles catching updrafts along the way. There are two other aspects of eagles that are noteworthy: 1. They build very large nests. Eagles never stop building. They continue to gather sticks, branches, leaves, and grass and add to their abode on a regular basis. I have seen nests that have been well over six feet in diameter and over two feet in thickness. They are continually adding to what they already have, making their home a fortress. 2. When the time comes for an eaglet to fly, the choice of staying in the nest is incrementally eliminated. The mother eagle, sensing her young one is of flying age, will begin to make the nest uncomfortable. She does this by bringing in thorns and stones and will leave bits of sharp bone on the floor of the nest. When all else fails, she will actually push her little one out of the nest and it will be given the abrupt choice of flying or dying. It may seem cruel to treat a young one this way, but all eagles understand this: Eagles are meant to fly, not lounge and relax in the comforts of a large nest.

In Isaiah 40:29-31 we read, "He gives strength to the weary, and to him who lacks might He increases power. Though youths grow weary and tired, and vigorous young men stumble badly, yet those who wait for the Lord will gain new strength; they will mount up with wings like eagles, they will run and not get tired, they will walk and not become weary."

You were meant to grow and become more than you are. Ask Him for strength and motivation. Ask Him for direction. Ask Him for companions. Then surrender to the wind of His Spirit and soar. You were meant to outdistance your past. You can grow!

SHARING PIECES:

How does your chronological age compare to your spiritual age?

Share a time in your life when you grew the most spiritually. What did it involve?

What is the number one truth that God is teaching you right now?

What are some of the tools you use to grow?

PRINCIPLE # 11
YOU CAN EXPERIENCE SUCCESS

"ALL MEN HAVE FEARS, BUT THE BRAVE PUT DOWN THEIR FEARS AND GO FORWARD, SOMETIMES TO DEATH, BUT ALWAYS TO VICTORY." -KING'S GUARD MOTTO IN ANCIENT GREECE

In the archives of the Charlie Brown comics you find a particularly relevant episode featuring Charlie and Linus. Charlie is practicing his archery skills. He shoots an arrow at the side of a barn. Then he walks up to it and draws a bulls-eye around the arrow. Of course Linus informs him that that is not the way to practice archery. Charlie responds, "I know, but this way it's a whole lot easier to be successful." Charlie understands the humorous adage, "If at first you don't' succeed, redefine success." The end result will be success, but it will be as unimpressive as Beethoven announcing that he is going to play chopsticks flawlessly.

It must be understood that no matter where you are in your journey and how much success you've experienced, there is always another level. You can always climb higher, go farther, and do greater things.

I spoke with Bruce Jenner shortly after the 1976 Olympics. He had won a gold medal and set the world record in the process. It was an amazing feat and he was labeled the greatest athlete in the world. After we chatted for a while, I asked him a very important question, "How come you pole vault off the wrong foot?" He was very surprised that I knew that. He explained how it was a bad habit that he had developed and that there was so much pressure to compete that he never went backwards to correct this very basic flaw. The point is, as great as his record setting performance was, he still could have done better. The same is true for all of us in every venue in which we find ourselves. There is always a higher point we can reach and we are born with a natural desire to climb, meet challenges, and achieve.

That is why communism fails and capitalism succeeds. When it is understood that there is only so far a person can go no matter how hard he works, the motivation for accomplishment diminishes and a *just get by* attitude is developed. Capitalism, however, is built on the concept of accelerated returns. Generally, if a person will work harder, he will realize more reward for his labor. It motivates him to find better ways of doing things in order to achieve more.

The part of the equation so many are missing is the infusion of God into the success formula. Proverbs 16:1-3 states, "The plans of the heart belong to man, but the answer of the tongue is from the Lord. All the ways of a man are clean in his own sight, but the Lord weighs the motives. Commit your works to the Lord and your plans will be established." The world looks solely at the results of our decisions, but God is looking at the motive behind the decision. The world looks at the *what* but God is looking at the *why* and *how.* I Samuel 16:7 states, "Man looks at the outward appearance but the Lord looks at the heart." God is the sieve we must pass all our plans through. Whether it is a decision about education, marriage, health, investments, vocation, business, or money, God's will must be sought out in order for us to make the best decision.

Some people are reaching for success but what they are struggling for cannot be obtained.

Allow me to submit to you four major reasons people do not experience success even though it is within their power to reach it.

1. Some have the wrong definition of success. Some people are reaching for success but what they are struggling for cannot be obtained. Their idea of success is to get *just a little bit more.* It is a definition that is based on comparison to what others have but it is illusive. It is always coupled with numbers, titles, or experiences. It reminds me of the farmer who said, "I don't want to own all the land in the county, just what's attached to mine." Proverbs 16:25 speaks to this, "There is a way that seems right to a man, but its end is the way of death." Proverbs 3:5-6 says, "Trust in the Lord with all your heart, and do not lean on your own understanding. In all your ways acknowledge Him and He will make your paths

straight." You've got to come to a God-based conclusion regarding the definition of success. With God, success falls more into the category of obedience than in gathering things.

2. Many are involved with improper planning. Some folks fail due to a lack of proper planning. I recently read a sign in a convenience store that said, "Failure to plan on your part does not constitute an emergency on my part." Some people do not succeed because they do not put the proper plans in place that would position them for success. Opportunities for success come but they miss them because they are not in the proper place to grab them.

3. A lack of belief that success is attainable. Some people simply don't believe that success is possible for them. They have lived in the mode of failure for so long that they do not see success as a possibility. When you deal with a situation long enough, you tend to get used to it. You accept it as your lot and you see life as having a glass ceiling. Because you have tried a few times and come away bruised, you have drawn the conclusion that the level you are on is the level you are meant to be so there is no sense in trying to move beyond it. These people either don't believe in themselves or they don't believe in the plan God has for their lives.

4. As hard as it may seem, there are some who really lack the basic desire to succeed. Some have concluded that they don't deserve success so they sabotage any chance of winning. Perhaps it is an aversion to expectations or the responsibility success brings. Whatever the reason, people walk away from jobs, relationships, and opportunities. I've seen people deliberately miss appointments, skip classes, and turn down interviews. All this because they don't believe they are entitled to succeed.

I saw this take place in a young girl on a university campus. She struggled with self-esteem issues the entire time I knew her. She just didn't feel that she was good enough for school, friends, or sports. She was a sophomore and informed me that she was dropping out of school to go into the military. I encouraged her to stay in school and earn her degree. The military would be there after she got her diploma. That way, if she still wanted to have a military career, she would do it as an officer and that would change her financial picture drastically. My advice fell on deaf ears. She wasn't interested in being successful and getting a head start, she was determined to sabotage any advantage she would have over anyone else.

There is a formula for success that each of us can initiate. It has to do with current resources we possess, needs we have, and the success that marrying these two categories will bring. The formula is simple:

2 + X = Success.

The number two is represented by the amount of resources you currently have. This number may be higher for some, but it is seen at the very least as two resources: Knowledge and experience. Some also have money, positions, and other resources.

X represents what is needed: Education, an introduction, marketing, production, finances, etc. all fall into this category.

When you add all these together, you have the greatest chance at success. It runs like this:

There is a cost to everything and you must make sure the benefit of having what you need in order to get what you want is worth the price you must pay for it.

2 (Knowledge, Experience) + X (What you need) = Success.

When considering what you need, it is helpful to evaluate the cost and place that against the benefit of having what you need. There is a cost to everything and you must make sure the benefit of having what you need in order to get what you want is worth the price you must pay for it. This is called a *cost/benefit analysis*. But please understand that no one can achieve greatness unless he is willing to hurt himself deeply. Success worth pursuing always encompasses struggles on some level.

In order to be successful you must be willing to marry inspiration with opportunity. What inspires you? Perhaps a person, a story, or a dream is what pushes you forward to seek a goal. There has to be something that will cause you to reach beyond where you are today in order to achieve more than you have. Along with being inspired, you must keep your eyes open to opportunities. Sometimes they come in the form of money, education, experience, time, or any number of other ways, but you must be open to seeing them and be willing to take advantage of them.

You have heard the comment, "quitting in not an option." I understand the motivation behind that phrase. What is being put forth is that we have to avoid exercising the option to quit. The truth is quitting is always an option. It is an option for all of us in everything we do. We see quitting exemplified all around us in marriage, jobs, athletics, education, the military, etc. The list of opportunities to quit is endless. What we must decide is whether or not what we are pursuing is worth the price we must pay to get it. Success always comes with a cost. The question becomes, is the benefit of what I'm after bigger than the struggle I must experience to get it? If it is concluded that it is not, then the option of quitting the pursuit looms ever larger. The fact is everyone faces the option of quitting. Those who succeed are the ones who don't exercise the option.

We are not all wired the same and what is seen as success to one person may not hold the same value to another.

You'll find that those who pressed beyond the barriers of quitting and succeeded ran a similar continuum where each level brings you to the next one. The ones who achieve the most are the ones who reach the last level:

1. THOUGHT: "That's Interesting!" → (Quit) or:

2. DESIRE: "I Want To Try That!" → (Quit) or:

3. EXPERIENCE: "Guess What I Did?" → (Quit) or:

4. TASTE (Evaluation): "I Like That!" → (Quit) or:

5. HUNGER: "I Want To Do That Again!" → (Quit) or:

6. CRAVING (Passion): → "Get Out Of My Way!"

As a follower of Christ, you'll find that there are certain keys to success. Turning each of those keys is the way to open the door to what God has planned for your life.

1. Define what success is for you. What is it that you feel would be a personal definition of success in a particular area? It must be something that is challenging, will grow you in your walk with Christ, and is personal. We are not all wired the same and what is seen as success to one person may not hold the same value to another. Perhaps success is memorizing a certain number of Bible verses, or passages of Scripture. Maybe for you it's owning your own company or moving into a certain position where you are employed. You might be interested in running a marathon or losing a certain amount of weight. It could be that you want to become a writer or learn a particular skill. Whatever excites you, you must be able to fill in the blank, "If I ____________________________, I will look at it as success.

2. Pray about it. This is crucial in the believer's life. Proverbs tells us, "There is a way that seems right to a man, but its end is the way of death" (Proverbs 14:12). God knows what you need to be successful in whatever endeavor you choose. He wants to see you succeed and be fulfilled. He longs to direct your life and show you the way you should go. But you must be willing to allow Him to make the rules and give you direction. The Bible tells us, "The steadfast of mind Thou wilt keep in perfect peace because he trusts in Thee" (Isaiah 26:3). God will direct your plans but you must let Him have the reins. He will show you what He wants you to pursue through His word, circumstances, people, and His Holy Spirit speaking directly to your heart. He expects you to set the sail and give the rudder to Him to determine the direction.

3. Seek wise council. Maybe others have gone before you pursuing what you desire. Follow the trail, and seek advice. They will tell you what to avoid and share with you possible shortcuts to your goal. They may even serve as a point of inspiration spurring you on beyond what you thought you could do. Proverbs 15:22 says, "Without consultation, plans are frustrated, but with many counselors they succeed."

4. Resist the temptation to compare yourself with anyone else. Remember this is your plan, desire, and definition of success. Comparison will only lead you to jealousy over someone else's achievements or pride over those you appear to be ahead of.

5. Plan for success. After defining success, praying about it, seeking council, and carrying the proper perspective regarding it, you must sit down and make your plans for success. This is the *How To* part of any adventure. This is where you will plug in what you have with what you need and find success as you have defined it.

You'll find that success is very difficult. If it doesn't involve some form of struggle, then the taste of it will not be as sweet. But you'll also find that the benefits of success are worth the price you must pay for it. All mountain climbers know the view is worth the climb. Success is worthy of your greatest effort. Success is reachable. You can be successful.

SHARING PIECES:

What would have to be in place in order for you to label your life a success?

How does the world's definition of success compare to your definition of success?

What do you think your pursuit of success will cost you?

What would you say is a "craving" for you?

PRINCIPLE #12
YOU CAN DEVELOP LASTING RELATIONSHIPS

"IS ANY PLEASURE ON EARTH AS GREAT AS A CIRCLE OF CHRISTIAN FRIENDS BY A FIRE?" -C.S. LEWIS

Study after study shows that the typical male over thirty does not have one genuine friend with whom he can reveal his true self and share his deepest innermost thoughts. That is so very sad and borders on pathetic. Why is it that in a world occupied by approximately eight billion people, that so many men (and women) live a life of self-imposed exile? In its basic form, friendlessness in many ways is a self-inflicted wound.

Most solid relationships are symbiotic in nature. That is to say there is a give and take on the part of each of the participants. This is demonstrated in nature when one looks at scenes of great hippo and rhino herds. On the back of these large beasts is often seen a very small bird. This bird is called a tick bird. It gets its name from the mainstay of its diet-ticks. The tick bird is built with a long curved beak with which it can dig between the folds of fat on the back of the rhinos and hippos. Death can occur when these large animals are infested with enough ticks. So these gigantic mammals supply ticks for the birds and the birds, in turn, rid their counterparts of the menacing ticks. This is the essence of a symbiotic relationship. The tick bird needs these animals to supply its meal and the animals need the tick bird to keep them clean and healthy. It is the proverbial win-win situation.

We humans are created to be relational. The creation of man begins with the statement of the God-head, "Let us make man in our image..." (Gen. 1:26). God is a plural being in that His essence is the Father, Son, and Holy Spirit. They exist in communion with one another and we are created in that same likeness and with similar personality traits as God. Originally, it was the God-head (three in one). Then came man and God. Next were man and woman. And finally, God, man, and woman. Again, three designed to live as one.

Notice also that the first chapter of Genesis is replete with a positive evaluation of creation. God created everything and labeled it *good.* The sun, moon, stars, land, sea, and everything else were called by God *good.* There is a change however in what God says after he creates man. In Genesis 1:31 He has completed his work with his crowning achievement by making man. And He labels it all *very good.* There is something about mankind that is special. He is the only part of creation that is created in the likeness of God. Also, he is the only part of creation that is commanded to rule over all the other creatures of the earth (Gen. 1:26). Further, he is the only part of creation to have his mate chosen for him and thereby commanded to be with her in the covenant of marriage. In Gen. 2:18, we find the first negative statement made in the history of the world. Keep in mind, that up to this point, everything was labeled *good* and *very good.* But here we see that there is something that is not good and it involves the special part of God's creation, man. "It is not good for the man to be alone…" This is not a command for each of us to be married. Paul states in I Cor. 7:8, "But I say to the unmarried and to the widows that it is good for them if they remain even as I." Rather than being a command for marriage, Genesis 2:18 is a statement of how we are made. We are created to be social beings and to live in communion with one another. There are times in our lives when solitude can be of great benefit. It can help up focus on God's design for our lives and regenerate our physical bodies as well as our minds. But a life of solitude falls outside of the plan of God. We are to be involved in one another's lives!

The Bible is full of examples of those who built relationships with others: Jonathan and David, Barnabus and John Mark, Paul and Silas, Ruth and Naomi, Moses and Jethro, Esther and Mordecai, Jesus and the Disciples are only a few of the myriad of relationships to which the Bible speaks. God's plan is for *us* to be with *us*!

The relationships we build vary and can be categorized into four basic levels centered around the communication we have with various people we encounter.

Level 1-Recognition. This is seen when we encounter a person we have seen before and perhaps quite often but we don't share any more than a *hello* or *good morning.*

Level 2-Information Exchange. This represents a relationship where we speak to another person but there is no depth to our conversation. We are just sharing information and little more than that. The time, weather, date, or score of the game are all that is communicated at this level.

Level 3-Opinions. On this level we start sharing our feelings regarding various topics. It may be political, educational, current events, or sports, but we enter into conversations with others based on our relationship with them.

Level 4-Feelings, dreams, experiences. On this level we've entered into a relationship where trust has been established and maintained. We feel free to invite the other person to hear and evaluate some aspects of our lives that may be highly personal and risky.

It can be immeasurably helpful to have a clear understanding of where you are in each of your relationships. It may establish boundaries for you and the other person as well as aid you in keeping expectations realistic.

In Ecclesiastes 4:9-12 we find a symbiotic relationship described between friends. Each of these verses can be developed into relational laws we can see at work. "Two are better than one because they have a good return for their labor. For if either of them falls, the one will lift up his companion. But woe to the one who falls when there is not another to lift him up. Furthermore, if two lie down together they keep warm, but how can one be warm alone? And if one can overpower him who is alone, two can resist him. A cord of three strands is not quickly torn apart."

Verse 9 involves the *Law of Synergy.* This means that together we can do more than each of us can do on our own. If two people can lift

100 pounds each on their own, the two combined can lift well over 200 pounds when working in concert with each other.

Working synergistically brings about many benefits:

A-It brings about encouragement. When someone is cheering for you and encouraging you to go on, you tend to go farther and do more than you were capable of doing on your own. Discouragement comes to us all, but it can be staved off a lot longer when you have someone beside you speaking life into you.

B-It fosters responsibility. If you know someone is counting on you, you will find few excuses not to do that which you are called to do. When a friend is coming over at seven a.m. on a Saturday morning to join you on a run, rolling over in bed is an option that is quickly eliminated.

C-It brings more minds to the table. You have the opportunity to look at things from various angles. There is more input to a project or problem. The more minds you have looking for a solution, the more options can be presented and perhaps the answer can come more quickly.

D-It adds to the enthusiasm. The more people involved in a worthwhile expedition, the more life you'll find in the camp. Not everyone can be *up* all the time so when there are more people involved, there is a greater chance of pulling each other along.

Verse 10 teaches the *Law of Safety*. Life is very complex and offers many opportunities for us to fall and struggle. Your friends are there to help you get up after a fall. They can help you stay out of trouble by advising you as you make decisions. Friends can also identify *blind spots* in your life and keep you from making big mistakes.

It's called the *buddy system* and it has saved many a life. The *buddy system* is used by swimmers, divers, hikers, scuba divers, mountain climbers and a host of others who put themselves in positions of danger. In short, the *buddy system* means no one goes alone. You always (and the word *always* is greatly emphasized), go with your buddy!

A humorous story is told about a young woman waiting for a bus in a dangerous part of a city one evening when a rookie policeman approached her. "Want me to wait with you?" he asked. She replied, "Thank you, but that's not necessary. I'm not afraid." "Well, then," he said grinning, "would you mind waiting with me?" That young officer understood the law of safety.

Verse 11 tells us of the *Law of Survival.* There are times in our lives when we simply have to launch ourselves into *survival mode*. It's not always about winning; sometimes it's about living through difficult times.

Hypothermia is a condition whereby the body has been exposed to cold temperatures for so long that its own ability to produce heat is not functioning. The person must gain body heat from a source outside itself. When climbers are stranded, it is often the practice of huddling together to conserve and exchange heat that saves their lives. If a person is in a condition of hypothermia and you wrap him in blankets to keep him warm, he will die. The idea is to introduce the body to an outside heat producing element. He needs someone else to be under the blanket with him providing the heat his body can't produce.

The relationships we build are a lot like that. Often we can't produce the *heat* needed for us to survive. That's where the warmth of good friends comes in. Good friends can side up next to you with a smile, a hug, a word of encouragement, or a warm hand shake. They can provide for you just what you need (and just when you need it) to survive. The old adage is true, "Encouragement is oxygen to the soul." Unknown

Verse 12 deals with the *Law of Security*. Great confidence occurs when you know someone *has your back*.

Years ago, the mother of one of our members had passed away and I was asked to conduct the funeral. There were two daughters involved, one of whom lived out of town and was coming in for the service. While preparing for the funeral, I was informed that the daughters had a very tough time growing up due to an abusive father. After years of physical and verbal abuse, he abandoned the family and had virtually no contact with them. The daughters were concerned that he would show up and made it clear that they didn't want him there. They didn't even want their mother's passing mentioned in the paper in case the father noticed it and showed up.

Somehow the father found out about it and attended. At the graveside, one of the daughters told the father in no uncertain terms that he was not welcome and that he should leave. He told her that he had a right to be there and was not going to leave. In stepping in, I told him that it was best for him not to be there and that if he wanted to visit later he could. This was not acceptable and he began to get demonstrative. I was concerned that he would become violent as his voice and mannerisms indicated. I told him that he was on private property and that he needed to go. Eventually, he turned and walked away. When I turned around, I was faced with three of my deacons. They had my back and were ready to jump in and defend me. That's what friends are for! They can be a great source of security for you.

Good friends help you get downwind of yourself and let you know when you're in need of a bath.

Friends can also be a great source of truth for you. They may tell you the truth even when you don't want to hear it. Good friends help you get *downwind* of yourself and let you know when you're in need of a bath. They can fill you in on information you need to have ranging anywhere from "your fly is down" to "you hurt a person's feelings and need to apologize." If we would simply be honest with ourselves, we would admit that we all have *blind spots* in our lives. These are areas that we pay little or no attention to because we think we've got it all together. But the truth is we're all just a collection of damaged parts working in the midst of a faulty machine called humanity. A good friend will lovingly tell you where your blind spot is and walk with you to remedy it. By listening closely, you can avoid many of the pitfalls that would otherwise come your way.

Proverbs 27:6 tells us, "Faithful are the wounds of a friend, but deceitful are the kisses of an enemy." In short, you are much better feeling the pain of correction from a caring friend than enjoying the accolades of one who really doesn't care for you. Take the hit from a friend! You'll be better for it!

True friendship always comes with a cost. There must be a mutual investment into the relationship if it's going to be healthy and fulfilling. The cost may come in the form of time, energy, money, experiences, or a plethora of other areas. But for the relationship to be all that it can be, both parties must be willing to give and receive from one another. Be that as it may, there is no question that deep friendships are worth the price of admission and maintenance.

Proverbs 18:24 tells us, "A man of many friends comes to ruin but there is a friend who sticks closer than a brother." It's speaking of those special relationships that we can build that give us a sense that we are closer than two brothers might be. It goes beyond family ties and common ancestry. Robert Brault said it so well, "I value the friend who for me finds time on his calendar, but I cherish the friend who for me does not consult his calendar."

Over time, people move in and out of your life. You grow close to them and revel in the relationship only to find that one of you must move on. It could be a job change, health issues, financial problems or a number of situations that causes the disruption of the friendship. This can be very disheartening. It can hurt deeply and make you feel lost and alone. But God has a way of making up for the losses in our lives. He has the ability to *backfill* into us with other people who will fill the gaps left by those who have moved on.

In Joel 1:4 we see a description of devastation that happened to the children of Israel. They needed to be disciplined by the hand of God and so He sent locusts to tear away their crops. There are two characteristics of locusts that make them devastating: They often come in huge swarms. These swarms can be so thick that they overshadow the sun and darken the sky. Besides their sheer numbers, they are relentless in their pursuit of food and they possess verocious appetites. Because of disobedience, God sent these destroyers of crops upon the land of His people. Follow the Bible's description of them; "What the gnawing locust has left, the swarming locust has eaten; and what the swarming locust has left, the creeping locust has eaten; and what the creeping locust has left, the stripping locust has eaten."

It sounds devastating, doesn't it? Sometimes the loss of a friendship can feel that way. We had a person who stuck closer than a brother only to have him taken to us by death or life issues. We feel lost and lonely and don't feel that we will ever have a friend (or friends) like that.

But the story is not over. What may take place next as we walk with the Lord is what I call *Locust Theology.* God has a way to make up for the losses in our lives. He can restore the hollow areas left by those who have moved on. Joel 2:25 speaks to this, "Then I will make up to you for the years that the swarming locust has eaten, the creeping locust, the stripping locust and the gnawing locust, my great army which I sent among you." In other words, all is not lost as long as God has a hand in it.

On more than one occasion, my wife and I have experienced *Locust Theology* first hand. We've suffered loss financially, professionally, physically, and socially. But we have witnessed the faithfulness of God in making up for the *swarming, creeping, stripping, gnawing* episodes in our lives.

My first job as an associate pastor was a great experience. I was to minister to the young married couples and families and the men of a large and growing church in Charlotte. It was a great position, and I learned and grew in leaps and bounds. On top of all that, I had served as a Sunday school teacher to the same age group as well as a deacon for a number of years. So to say that we built some great friendships over the years would be a gross understatement.

But the Lord began to stir in my heart His desire for me to pastor a church. God began to speak to me in several ways but because of our great circle of friends, I wasn't listening very well. God prevailed however, and it came time for us to move. This was so hard, so very hard. We had developed such great friendships over the years. We prayed together, played together, watched each other's children be born, and went shoulder to shoulder through so many difficult times.

Still, God is God. And He is Lord over all, including our relationships. So we answered the call and began a new chapter in ministry. Upon leaving, we really felt like the locusts had eaten all that we had sown into the lives of so many. Before long, however, God began to bring new friends our way in droves. We developed great relationships on so many levels and have grown in our love for the people God placed in our lives. God has indeed made up for the years it seems that the locusts have devoured. Anyone who is blessed with the great friends we've had truly understands how good God is regarding the provision of friendships.

Years ago, Sam Walter Foss found himself alone walking down a dusty road in New England. He stopped to rest beneath a tree. There beside him he found a sign reading: "Here is a spring, if thirsty, drink."

Moving down the road he came to a bench. It too had a sign which read, "If weary, rest on this bench."

Later, he came to a basket filled with apples. On the basket was a small sign saying, "If hungry, help yourself."

Down the road he arrived at an old hut. An old man was sitting on the porch. The old man cried out, "The blessings of the day to you!" Foss asked the old man the motivation for such great kindness and was told, "God gives great joy and I share what I have with others."

This led Sam Walter Foss to pen the words to the famous poem, *The House By The Side of The Road:*

There are hermit souls that live withdrawn

In the place of their self-content;

There are souls like stars, that dwell apart,

In a fellowless firmament;

There are pioneer souls that blaze the paths
Where highways never ran-
But let me live by the side of the road
And be a friend to man.

Let me live in a house by the side of the road
Where the race of men go by-
The men who are good and the men who are bad,
As good and as bad as I.
I would not sit in the scorner's seat
Nor hurl the cynic's ban-
Let me live in a house by the side of the road
And be a friend to man.

I see from my house by the side of the road
By the side of the highway of life,
The men who press with the ardor of hope,
The men who are faint with the strife,
But I turn not away from their smiles and tears,
Both parts of an infinite plan-
Let me live in a house by the side of the road
And be a friend to man.

I know there are brook-gladdened meadows ahead,

And mountains of wearisome height;
That the road passes on through the long afternoon
And stretches away to the night.
And still I rejoice when the travelers rejoice
And weep with the strangers that moan,
Nor live in my house by the side of the road
Like a man who dwells alone.

Let me live in my house by the side of the road,
Where the race of men go by-
They are good, they are bad, they are weak, they are strong,
Wise, foolish - so am I.
Then why should I sit in the scorner's seat,
Or hurl the cynic's ban?
Let me live in my house by the side of the road
And be a friend to man.

That, my friend, is the secret vitamin that develops friendships. It's called vitamin *Be-One*. To have a friend, you must be a friend. You must be loyal and trustworthy and willing to pay the price your friendship requires. You must give a sense of always being available and willing to share of your resources. You have to be an ear that will listen, a hand that will help, legs that will arrive and possess a heart that will just as easily laugh as cry.

To have a friend, you must be a friend. You must be loyal and trustworthy and willing to pay the price your friendship requires.

A dear friend of mine sent this piece of poetry my way and I received it in the spirit in which it was given:

"THANK GOD FOR YOU"

Thank God for you, good friend of mine,

Seldom is friendship such as thine;

How very much I wish to be

As helpful as you've been to me.

When I recall, from time to time,

How you inspired this heart of mine;

I find myself inclined to pray,

God bless my friend this very day.

So often, at the throne of grace,

There comes a picture of your face;

And then, instinctively, I pray,

That God may guide you all the way.

Some day, I hope with you to stand,

Before the throne, at God's right hand.

And say to you at journey's end;

Praise God, you've been to me a friend.

Thank God for You!

Let me close this chapter with a couple of queries:

- » Are you thankful for your friends and do you let them know?
- » Are you investing yourself in such a way that others are thankful for you?

SHARING PIECES:

Outside of your spouse, who is your best friend and what makes you label this person so?

Name three people who are on your "Inner circle" list.

When you experienced a deep struggle in your life, who was there for you?

Share a time when someone spoke the truth in love to you. How did you receive it?

PRINCIPLE # 13
YOU CAN EXPERIENCE PEACE AND JOY

"WE PRESS ON...SEEKING HAPPINESS EVER MORE ARDENTLY, AND FINDING DESPAIR EVER MORE ABUNDANTLY." -MALCOLM MUGGERIDGE

Do you think Jesus was joyful? A man of peace ("the Prince of Peace") we get, but joyful? Some are not so sure about that one. Can you picture Jesus laughing with the disciples? Can you see one of them bringing up a conversation or telling a joke and Jesus sitting down with laughter? Some people struggle with the idea of Jesus enjoying a good belly laugh. Some might even think it sacrilegious or blasphemous to suggest just such a scene. But I have no trouble seeing that happen. We are made in the image of God. And because this is true, we have certain personality traits, emotions, and a free will just like God. Humor comes from God. Not the crass, rude style we've made it out to be but the open honest ability to find humor in the ridiculous. We can laugh at things that strike us a certain way and find joy in some of the simplest of things.

There is peace to be had in the storm. There is joy in the midst of the heartache. There is safety in the center of danger. There is hope that overcomes despair.

Years ago, I came across a drawing titled "The Delightful Christ." It pictures Jesus with a grin that bespeaks of His just finishing a good laugh. I am told that the artist drew this in reflection of the resurrection as if it was the grandest practical joke that could ever be played on the devil. Sometimes when life gets particularly heavy, I'm drawn to that picture and it helps me put things in perspective.

Life can be very difficult. I don't deny it. But it is possible to experience peace and joy even when nothing seems to be going your way and you are in the center of struggles. There is peace to be had in the storm. There is joy in the midst of the heartache. There is safety in the center of danger. There is hope that overcomes despair.

"There is no box made by us or by God but that the top can be blown off and the sides flattened out to create a dance floor on which to celebrate life." -Tim Kimmel/Kenneth Caraway

This is what is communicated in Habakkuk 3:17-19. "Though the fig tree should not blossom and there be no fruit on the vines, though the yield of the olive should fail and the fields produce no food, though the flock should be cut off from the fold and there be no cattle in the stalls, yet I will exult in the Lord, I will rejoice in the God of my salvation. The Lord God is my strength, and He has made my feet like hinds' feet, and makes me walk on my high places."

Quite often peace, and in particular joy, get confused with happiness, even to the point where they are used interchangeably. People pursue happiness in order to experience joy with the desired end result being peace in their lives. But happiness is determined by *happenings* while peace and joy can stand independent of one's station in life or individual circumstances. While accumulating things or experiences can bring momentary satisfaction, peace and joy may not be present. It is similar to the ironic position of being lonely in a crowd. It is possible to have a lot to live on but not much to live for. And happiness evaporates with the loss of material goods or the end of the adventure.

Our world is replete with people who have a deep sense of peace and joy amid some very difficult circumstances. While in college, I met and became friends with one of them.

I was blessed with the opportunity to be a college athlete and participate on the track team for four years. In my freshman year our assistant coach, Jim Wright, brought his neighbor out to practice one day. His name was Wayne Vincent Cline but we called him Waynie. Waynie was twenty-four-years-old and was mentally challenged. But he became part of the team and even traveled with us to many of our meets. Waynie was friendly to everyone and talked incessantly. He had an eye for the ladies and was never shy about talking with them. Often, I would get a phone call from Waynie asking me how I was and if I was ready to win again. What a great outlook from a young man whose circumstances did not dictate his joy and peace.

On this topic, I am compelled to share with you the story of Lou "Iron Horse" Gehrig. His life was anything but perfect and it ended at the early age of thirty-seven. He was born in E. Harlem, N.Y. to German immigrants who struggled to make ends meet. His father was often jobless and his mother had to work as a maid and became the main breadwinner. His two sisters died of whooping cough and the measles. His brother died in infancy.

Yet he went on to become a major league baseball player playing all seventeen years of his career with the New York Yankees. But in 1939 he was diagnosed with Amyotrophic Lateral Sclerosis, a disease that would end his life on June 2, 1941. The Yankees proclaimed July 4, 1939 as Lou Gehrig Appreciation day. Standing before a crowd of over 61,000 fans Gehrig offered this iconic speech:

> Fans, for the past two weeks you have been reading about the bad break I got. Yet today I consider myself the luckiest man on the face of the earth. I have been in ballparks for seventeen years and have never received anything but kindness and encouragement from you fans.
>
> Look at these grand men. Which of you wouldn't consider it the highlight of career just to associate with them for even one day? Sure, I'm lucky. Who wouldn't consider it an honor to have known Jacob Ruppert? Also, the builder of baseball's greatest empire, Ed Barrow? To have spent six years with that wonderful little fellow, Miller Huggins? Then to have spent the next nine years with that outstanding leader, that smart student of psychology, the best manager in baseball today, Joe McCarthy? Sure, I'm lucky.
>
> When the New York Giants, a team you would give your right arm to beat, and vice versa, sends you a gift — that's something. When everybody down to the groundskeepers and those boys in white coats remember you with trophies — that's something.

> When you have a wonderful mother-in-law who takes sides with you in squabbles with her own daughter — that's something. When you have a father and a mother who work all their lives so that you can have an education and build your body — it's a blessing. When you have a wife who has been a tower of strength and shown more courage than you dreamed existed — that's the finest I know.
>
> So I close in saying that I might have been given a bad break, but I've got an awful lot to live for. Thank you.

How can a man who was given such a poor start in life and whose career and life had been cut mercilessly short come to the conclusion that he was the luckiest man alive? Could it have been because he learned the secret of separating joy and peace which is a state of mind from happiness which is a state of circumstances?

In Luke 12:16-21, Jesus tells the parable of the rich fool.

> *And He told them a parable, saying, The land of a certain rich man was very productive. And he began reasoning to himself, saying, "What shall I do, since I have no place to store my crops?" And he said, "This is what I will do: I will tear down my barns and build larger ones, and there I will store all my grain and my goods. And I will say to my soul, 'soul, you have many goods laid up for many years to come; take your ease, eat, drink and be merry.'" But God said to him, "you fool! This very night your soul is required of you; and now who will own what you have prepared?" So is the man who lays up treasure for himself, and is not rich toward God.*

This is the only occurrence where we find Jesus labeling a man a fool. He is not a fool because he has money. He is not a fool because he has worked hard. He is not a fool because he has saved. He is a fool for two very basic reasons. He speaks only to himself. He is not approaching God to see what it is the creator of the universe would have him do. He speaks only inwardly to his soul. Also, note that he has come to a very dangerous conclusion. He has decided that money and things are synonymous with joy, peace, and long life. That's the problem we face when we pursue things as a means of finding joy and peace. We chase them and wear ourselves out in the hunt, but when we finally capture them, we find emptiness and disappointment.

Recently, I shared a meal with a good friend of mine. He is a businessman and has done extremely well in industry. In a moment of reflection he related his perspective on all that he has. He said, "If God took it all away tomorrow, I would still be okay because I know that that is not where my fulfillment lies."

Jesus said, "Peace I leave with you; My peace I give to you; not as the world gives, do I give to you. Let not your heart be troubled, nor let it be fearful." (John 14:27). Did you catch what the Master was saying? He gives peace. He gives His peace. And the peace that He gives is not the same as the peace the world gives. You'll find that the world's attempt at bringing peace will be external. It will come by way of things or experiences. But the world does not have the capability to bring about the peace that God can bring. God brings peace to us internally. It comes to our souls and extends out to our physical being. It is a unique peace that is delivered outside of our circumstances and can come even in the midst of the most difficult of times. Regarding peace, the Apostle Paul said, "And the peace of God, which surpasses all comprehension, shall guard your hearts and your minds in Christ Jesus." (Philippians 4:7). This means that the peace that only God can bring will go beyond your understanding. Life will come at you in very harsh ways. In the midst of the loss of loved ones, unemployment, health issues, betrayal, and disappointment, God can bring His peace. And having His peace while experiencing all this trouble will go beyond what you or anybody else can understand. Psalm 30:5b tells us, "Weeping may last for the night. But a shout of joy comes in the morning." It's a God thing!

Years ago two artists were asked to paint a scene with the theme of peace. One artist filled the canvas with a rolling hillside and a beautiful lake in the foreground. The sun was shining, several sheep were grazing, and birds filled the sky. It was a beautiful picture of peace. But the scene that stole the eye of the critics was very different. It was the scene of a storm. The branch of a tree hung over a raging river with the wind blowing fiercely and lightning streaking across a black sky. The overhanging branch held a small bird's nest. In the nest was a mother bird with her wings spread out over her brood of three sleeping birds. In the midst of the torrent, those three birds were experiencing peace. That is a picture of what the Master was offering to those who followed Him. It is not freedom from pain and struggle, but peace and joy in the midst of trial.

It is very difficult to grab hold of joy and peace on a permanent basis. Certain aspects of life can steal our joy and block our peace. You'll find that the two areas that will truncate both of these are people and our own minds.

People: The people that come and go in our lives can be our greatest asset or our biggest struggle. *Sometimes it can be the same person.* These folks generally fall into two categories: the "Field Stumps" and the critics.

Field Stumps: If you have ever spent time driving in the country and looked out over a farmer's field, often you can locate a field stump. A field stump is simply that. It is a stump of a tree that is found in a field. The farmer working the field knows that a field stump is a formidable obstacle. It is large and it is in his way. But a farmer knows he has two options: he can hit the field stump with his plow every time he makes a pass, or he can simply plow around it. A wise farmer will choose to plow around the field stump. He will be patient and allow the elements of wind, rain, and erosion to have their way with the field stump. Then finally, over a long period of time, the stump will be rotted away and will be turned under the soil and be used to fertilize the very field in which it caused such problems.

The metaphor regarding people is easy to see. Field stumps in our lives are those who come our way and always bring up why a program, plan, or idea just won't work. They often don't offer a suggestion or a helping hand, but they are quick to inform you and anyone else who will listen, that your idea is not going to work. Sometimes they will go out of their way to discredit you or sabotage your project. It's not easy, but it is necessary that we plow around the people who are field stumps in our lives and we allow the elements of God's hand to work in the lives of those who present themselves as field stumps. God has a way of working that goes far beyond our wisdom or abilities. He will work behind the scenes and below the surface even at the soul level to prevent these people from blocking our joy and peace. He may even remove them and cause them to be a point of strength for our lives.

Critics: People often come our way in the form of critics. Somehow these people have become the self-appointed judges who stand to rule on everything we say and do. But if we are to walk in joy and experience God's peace, we must not let them establish a stronghold on our hearts. This is no small task. As a preacher and pastor I've had my struggles with those who would sit at the judge's bench. I've been criticized for my sermons, schedule, annunciation, leadership, friendships, plans, programs, attitude, decisions, ad infinitum, ad nauseam. Somehow, there is a tendency to think that when one person complains or criticizes, it is representative of the majority. That's just what the critic wants you to believe, but it is quite often not true. You must not succumb to the *croaking frogs* mentality. Just before evening it is quite common for the frogs inhabiting a pond to begin their regular ritual of croaking. When one starts, others join in and before long there is a cacophony of croaking going on that can be almost deafening. When you pay attention to all that noise (all they're really saying is "I'm available"), you think that there are hundreds of frogs in the pond. But in reality a relatively small number make all that racket. This is similar to what we experience when we analyze the voices of the critics. Their numbers are usually much less than we have concuded.

If not careful, one can find oneself spending all his time answering and trying to please the critics.

There is an old adage that I learned long ago and I've implemented it quite often in my ministry. It helps me to stay focused and on task. The *dogs bark, but the caravan moves on*. We must find a way to avoid letting the voices of the critics drown out the truth of our lives and situation. Negative events occur in our lives and we have a tendency to conclude that it is indicative of other areas and that *all is bad.*

In Dr. Henry Cloud's book *Necessary Endings* he describes a condition known as learned-helplessness.

> For instance, when someone doesn't get a sale, it means 'I am a loser, the whole business is bad, and it isn't going to change.' These are called by Seligman and others the three P's. Events are processed in predictable, negative ways: first, as *personalized* (I am a bad salesperson); second, as *pervasive* (everything I do, or every aspect of the business, is bad); and third, as *permanent* (nothing is going to change). You can easily see why this leads to helplessness and inactivity.

If not careful, one can find oneself spending all his time answering and trying to please the critics. But Winston Churchill advises, "You will never reach your destination if you stop and throw stones at every dog that barks." If our plans are from the mind of God and our goal is to please Him, then we must find a way to push beyond the critics and not allow them to steal our joy and peace.

Having joy and peace drained from our lives may also emanate from ourselves. This may be more difficult to avoid because so often we are our worst enemy. We can ignore the critics and plow around the field stumps, but how do you get away from you? No matter where you go you're there!

Intrinsically, you'll find that the source of our internal struggle will come from four major areas: Lack of trust, worry, unforgiveness of ourselves or others, and selfishness.

Lack of trust: Anything less than total faith in God falls on the side of lack of trust. God wants us to be able to trust Him with all aspects of our lives and to place our faith in Him not just for our eternal salvation, but for day to day living. He is not just the God of the "sweet by and by." He is also the God of the "nasty here and now." Trust is always placed somewhere. When it is not placed in God, it is either placed on someone else or ourselves. To place our trust anywhere other than God is to put ourselves in hands that we know have failed us (most times repeatedly). But God has never failed us. We must be careful not to place the label failure on the fact that we did not get our way. What it simply means is that God has a better plan for us.

Hermann Lange understood this. On July 11, 1943 he faced execution by the Nazis with this reflection, "Personally, I am perfectly calm, facing steadfastly what is to come. When one has really achieved complete surrender to the will of God, there is a marvelous feeling of peace and sense of absolute security. The gift we receive is so unimaginably great that all human joys pale beside it."

Worry: The twin brother of a lack of trust is worry. Worry is spawned by a lack of trust and is a code word for fear. Worry is what you get when you develop the habit of not trusting God. Worry is the enemy of progress. It will make you lose sleep, friends, appetite, energy, and years off your life. Arthur Somers Roche notes, "Worry is a thin stream of fear trickling through the mind. If encouraged, it cuts a channel into which all other thoughts are drained." Worrying is non-productive and serves absolutely no purpose.

Jesus tells us in Luke 12:22-28,

> For this reason I say to you, do not be anxious for your life, as to what you shall eat; nor for your body, as to what you shall put on. For life is more than food, and the body more than clothing. Consider the ravens, for they neither sow nor reap; and they have no storeroom, nor barn; and yet God feeds them; how much more valuable you are than the birds! And which of you by being anxious can add a single cubit to his life's span? If then you cannot do even a very little thing, why are you anxious about other matters? Consider the lilies, how they grow; they neither toil nor spin; but I tell you, even Solomon in all his glory did not clothe himself like one of these. But if God so arrays the grass in the field, which is alive today and tomorrow is thrown into the furnace, how much more will He clothe you O men of little faith. And do not seek what you shall eat, and what you shall drink, and do not keep worrying.

No matter how many times you read that you must come up with the same conclusion. Jesus is giving a directive. DO NOT WORRY!

Victor Hugo offers this advice, *Have courage for the great sorrows of life and patience for the small ones; and when you have laboriously accomplished your daily task, go to sleep in peace. God is awake.*

If however, you are in the habit of worrying, it will take great effort to move from what you so naturally default to toward confidently walking in faith and trust. But the rewards of doing so far outdistance any strange comfort and pleasure you get by worrying. Chuck Swindoll phrases it this way, "The happiest people I know are the ones who have learned how to hold everything loosely and have given the worrisome, stress-filled, fearful details of their lives into God's keeping."

You must identify the area of your life in which you don't trust God. Is it worry that has led you to a lack of trust? Do you feel that you have better control of your life and circumstances than Almighty God? What will it take to cause you to totally surrender to the control of the creator of the universe? How loudly does God have to speak to you to get you to let go of the steering wheel and allow Him to direct where you will go and how quickly?

Unforgiveness: Another open drain line to our peace and trust is unforgiveness. There are two sources of unforgiveness that we all have to deal with: Withholding forgiveness from others and doing the same for ourselves. When we refuse to forgive others, we commit two violations. We put ourselves in the place of God (and that never ends well), and we misevaluate our own lives by thinking that our sins are not nearly as bad and therefore we have a right not to forgive.

Not receiving forgiveness leads to two problems: When we decide that our sin is too great for God to forgive, we *lower* the value of the life, death, and resurrection of the Lord Jesus. We have decided that His blood and power cannot possibly cover our violation. When we refuse to accept forgiveness from ourselves, we *elevate* our position over God's and decide that although God can forgive us, we can't forgive ourselves. Each of these positions has a crippling effect on us and can stop us from having the impact that God desires for our life.

Selfishness: Selfish people, and we all know some of them, never seem to be at peace and struggle to really enjoy the experiences they have or the things they possess. They place themselves at the center of the universe and think that the worst offense anyone can commit would be to disrupt their desire for happiness. Unfortunately, many times, they have concluded that peace and happiness can be found by possessing things.

So they spend all their time working to gain things at the expense of that which lasts and brings satisfaction. They give up family, friends, enriching experiences, and opportunities in order to gather for themselves more of what they already have. And in the end they don't discover peace and happiness; they find emptiness and isolation. Life itself loses its shine and they are left in despair. They echo the heartfelt feelings of Solomon in Ecclesiastes 1:2, "Vanity of vanities, says the preacher, vanity of vanities! All is vanity."

Peace and joy are emotions and just like other emotions (love, anger, fear); you have a choice to experience them or not. No one can make you happy. And no one can make you sad. Those emotions come your way by choice.

The condition in which selfish people often find themselves is also depicted very well in Haggai 1:5-6, "Now therefore thus says the Lord of hosts, consider your ways!" In other words, pay attention to what is going on around you. "You have sown much, but harvest little; you eat, but there is not enough to be satisfied; you drink, but there is not enough to become drunk; you put on clothing, but no one is warm enough; and he who earns, earns wages to put into a purse with holes." People who only look to their own needs never seem to find satisfaction, and joy and peace are elusive to them.

It is possible, however, to experience joy and peace as a hallmark of your life. I'm not talking about living your life like a bobble head and denying reality. I'm talking about developing an attitude and outlook that allows you to sleep in a storm and smile through the pain that life brings you.

1-Avoid the thieves that rob you of peace and joy. As we've seen, some are internal and some are external. Although you may not be able to eliminate them completely from your life, you may be able to side-step encounters with them and at the very least limit your time with them.

2-Make a determined decision to experience peace and joy. Peace and joy are emotions and just like other emotions (love, anger, fear); you have a choice to experience them or not. No one can make you happy. And no one can make you sad. Those emotions come your way by choice. Joy and peace are yours to be had by your own choosing. George Fields, the musical comedian, once said, "I'm in the category of being an *inverted paranoid.* Every morning when I wake up I get this sneaky suspicion that someone is out to do me good." The choice to be joyful and at peace is truly yours to make.

3-Develop the proper perspective about life. Jesus said, "I came that they might have life and might have it abundantly." (John 10:10b). This is not a promise of abundance, but a promise of abundant living. Abundant living is full living. It's a life filled with hope and meaning. It's a life that seeks to help others. It's a life that seeks the face of God in everything you do. It's recognizing the blessings that come your way, turning your face up toward the Master, and whispering a deep and heartfelt thanks.

A friend of mine was on a summer long mission trip to South America. While there, she stayed with a family in a village. By almost every standard, this family was poor. They had almost no income, no running water, no indoor heating or cooling, and were not sure about where their next meal would come from. Yet my friend has labeled them the happiest people she has ever met. They don't waste time thinking about what they don't have. They are grateful for what the Lord has given them and are more than willing to share. They share everything from food, to clothes, to stories. They help each other to gather food and firewood. They hug and smile. Each night, their tiny front porch is filled with laughter, and singing and peace and joy reign triumphant in their hearts.

Years ago, I came across this piece of poetry attributed to Red Foley that sums up the importance of a proper perspective,

"GOD, FORGIVE ME WHEN I WHINE."

Today I saw upon a bus

A lovely maid with golden hair;

I envied her- she seemed so fair

And , oh, I wished I was so fair

When suddenly she rose to leave,

I saw her hobble down the aisle;

She had one foot and wore a crutch,

But as she passed, a smile.

Oh, God, forgive me when I whine;

I have two feet- the world is mine.

And when I stopped to buy some sweets,

The lad who served me had such charm

He seemed to radiate good cheer;

His manner was so kind and warm.

I said, "It's nice to deal with you;

Such courtesy I seldom find"

He turned and said, "Oh thank you"

And then I saw - He was blind.

Oh, God, forgive me when I whine;
I have two eyes - the world is mine

Then, when walking down the street,
I saw a child with eyes so blue
He stood and watched the others play;
It seemed he knew not what to do.
I stopped a moment, and then I said:
"why don't you join the others, Dear?"
he looked ahead without a word,
and then I knew - He could not hear.

Oh, God, forgive me when I whine
I have two ears - the world is mine.

With two feet to take me where I'd go,
With eyes to see the sunset's glow,
With ears to hear what I should know,
I'm blessed indeed; the world is mine
Oh, God, forgive me when I whine!

4-Develop directives for your life. Spend some time thinking about things that mean something to you and write them down. Then put those priorities into a form of directives that you have determined will frame your life. Allow me to share four of my directives with you:

A-I will laugh every day. Life is too short and people are too funny, not to develop laughter wrinkles. Do you realize that laughter comes from God? God has a sense of humor (I know He gets a laugh out of some of the things I do). I'm talking about good humor, not what we've done in labeling crass and sinful behavior funny. I'm talking about the ridiculous situations we put ourselves in. Stop taking yourself too seriously and enjoy the gift of laughter that comes from God.

B-I will encourage someone every day. Encouragement is food for the soul and too many people are malnourished. Encouragement can come in the form of a warm smile, a firm handshake, a loving hug, a note, a call, a text, or a gift. The avenues and opportunities are endless. Because I understand the value of encouragement, I have assumed the position of "CEO" for our church. "CEO" stands for Chief Encouragement Officer.

C-I will do my best to live in the center of God's will every day. I don't always do this well. I'm a damaged product just like everyone else. But my motivation is to follow God's leading in everything I do every day as best as I can approximate it. Through God's word, God's people, circumstances, and His Spirit living in me, I do the best I can to follow His leading. When I blow it, I go to Him as soon as I'm aware of it and confess and clear the slate between us. Being in the center of His will means that I must deny myself, take up my cross daily, and follow Him. (Luke 9:23). On the practical level, I must let go of my emotions, my will, my schedule and plans, my wallet, and my relationships. I must simply say "Yes, Lord!" Somehow we've gotten the idea that to follow Christ is to make out our daily list of things we feel we should do and take it to the Lord for His signature of approval. But actually the opposite is true. What a follower of Christ must do is sign a blank piece of paper every day and take it to the Lord for Him to fill in the details.

D-I will endeavor to take as many people to heaven as I can. After our salvation experience, we are left on earth for one purpose and one purpose only. That is to witness to God's love and mercy, while we try to convince those around us to accept Him and become children of God. Some would argue that our purpose is to spend our lives in praise to Him. Others would say that our purpose is to obey Him. Still others would contend that we are to be busy loving Him. These are all part of the plan, but heaven holds all these activities in abundance. We will spend eons of time praising Him. We'll live in eternal obedience to Him. All of heaven will be filled with His love. What we will not do in heaven is evangelize. We will not be leading anyone to a saving relationship with Christ. Our time on earth is to live with the salvation of others motivating our actions.

Joseph Addison has said, "The grand essentials of happiness in this life are something to do, someone to love, and something to hope for."

5-Discover something to do, something to love, and something to hope for. People whose lives are adorned with joy and peace have these three elements woven throughout their lives.

A-Something to do. Let me remind you that Goethe completed Faust at age eighty. Titian painted masterpieces at age ninety-eight. Toscanini still conducted at age eighty-five. Justice Holmes wrote Supreme Court decisions while ninety years old. Edison was busy in his laboratory when he was eighty-four. And Benjamin Franklin helped frame the American Constitution at the age of eighty.

A well-known story is often shared about an eighty-seven year old woman named Rose who went back to school. The story is told through the eyes of a young man who was influenced deeply by her:

The first day of school our professor introduced himself and challenged us to get to know someone we didn't already know.

I stood up to look around when a gentle hand touched my shoulder. I turned around to find a wrinkled, little old lady beaming up at me with a smile that lit up her entire being.

She said, "Hi handsome. My name is Rose. I'm eighty-seven years old. Can I give you a hug?"

I laughed and enthusiastically responded, "Of course you may!" and she gave me a giant squeeze.

"Why are you in college at such a young, innocent age?" I asked.

She jokingly replied, "I'm here to meet a rich husband, get married, and have a couple of kids…"

"No seriously," I asked. I was curious what may have motivated her to be taking on this challenge at her age.

"I always dreamed of having a college education and now I'm getting one!" she told me.

After class we walked to the student union building and shared a chocolate milk shake. We became instant friends. Every day for the next three months, we would leave class together and talk nonstop. I was always mesmerized listening to this "time machine" as she shared her wisdom and experience with me.

Over the course of the year, Rose became a campus icon and she easily made friends wherever she went. She loved to dress up and she reveled in the attention bestowed upon her from the other students. She was living it up.

At the end of the semester we invited Rose to speak at our football banquet. I'll never forget what she taught us. She was introduced and stepped up to the podium.

As she began to deliver her prepared speech, she dropped her three by five cards on the floor. Frustrated and a little embarrassed she leaned into the microphone and simply said, "I'm sorry I'm so jittery. I gave up beer for Lent and this whiskey is killing me! I'll never get my speech back in order so let me just tell you what I know."

As we laughed she cleared her throat and began, "We do not stop playing because we are old; we grow old because we stop playing. There are only four secrets to staying young, being happy, and achieving success. You have to laugh and find humor every day.

You've got to have a dream. When you lose your dreams, you die.

We have so many people walking around who are dead and don't even know it! There is a huge difference between growing older and growing up.

If you are nineteen years old and lie in bed for one full year and don't do one productive thing, you will turn twenty years old.

If I am eighty-seven years old and stay in bed for a year and never do anything I will turn eighty-eight.

Anybody can grow older. That doesn't take any talent or ability. The idea is to grow up by always finding opportunity in change.

Have no regrets.

The elderly usually don't have regrets for what we did, but rather for things we did not do. The only people who fear death are those with regrets."

She concluded her speech by courageously singing "The Rose."

She challenged each of us to study the lyrics and live them out in our daily lives.

At the year's end Rose finished the college degree she had begun all those years ago. One week after graduation Rose died peacefully in her sleep.

Over two thousand college students attended her funeral in tribute to the wonderful woman who taught by example that it's never too late to be all you can possibly be .

Remember, growing older is mandatory. Growing up is optional.

Rose found something to do with her life and it added fulfillment to her years.

B-Something to love-When you get outside of yourself and your own world filled with selfish desires, you discover the wonderful ability to love someone. Love is not something that diminishes as we share it. It is simply multiplied as we give it away. It's similar to a candle. If we light a candle and use it to light someone else's candle, we don't lose any of the original light we had. We are simply transferring some of the light while maintaining all the light we possessed.

If we light a candle and use it to light someone else's candle, we don't lose any of the original light we had. We are simply transferring some of the light while maintaining all the light we possessed.

C-Something to hope for-We all need something to hope for. That's what makes life worth living. That's why encouragement is so vital to the lives of those with whom we come in contact.

Interesting enough, each of those elements can be found in abundance in a personal relationship with Jesus Christ. Jesus will give you something to do. The harvest *is* plentiful, but the workers are few. (Matthew 9:37). Kingdom work is its own reward. Jesus, because of who He is and what He's done, beckons us to love Him. Jesus will give you something to hope for. His approval and the rewards of heaven are the center of the hope of the Christian life.

6-Understand and enjoy your relationship with God. The Westminster catechism states, *Man's chief end is to glorify God and to enjoy Him forever*. When we see what we've been rescued from and what we've been saved for, gratitude can only follow. God has great plans for us. Jeremiah 29:11, tells us, "For I know the plans I have for you, declares the Lord, plans for welfare and not for calamity to give you a future and a hope." What comfort we find in those words. What hope they give the follower of God. What optimism springs from a heart that takes God at His word and trusts Him with his future!

God has great plans for us. They are plans created in the mind of an infinite, all-knowing, all-powerful God. God wants better things for us than we want for ourselves and the plans He has for us are better than the plans we have for ourselves. His plans include complete forgiveness of sin and life eternal with Him in heaven. It cannot get any better than that!

The problem so many of us have is that we fail to understand fully who we are and who God is and where we stand in our relationship with Him. Until we pull that into focus, we will not be able to fully enjoy our relationship with Him. That in turn will affect how we think about ourselves and how we act around others In some of the darkest days of our country when we were involved in the buying and selling of slaves, an incident occurred that illustrates the importance of knowing who we are. A young slave trader stood alongside a seasoned trader and watched as an entire village was chained and marched toward awaiting ships. Life for them would never be the same. He heard the people crying and wailing. He watched the people fight against the chains and the captors. He saw the fear and despair in the eyes of the soon to be slaves. Yet in the midst of it all, he noticed a young man standing tall with his head held high. He picked his feet up as he walked and held his chains up in front of him. His pride and calm demeanor were easily evident. Having witnessed this, the young slave trader questioned the older man regarding this one individual. The reply spoke volumes about the captive. "He behaves the way he does because he is the son of the king."

If you have trusted Christ as your Savior, you are a child of the king and have every reason to hold your head high and live with the assurance of eternal glory.

Because of what Christ has done for us, we each have the opportunity to be sons and daughters of the King of Kings and Lord of Lords! John 1:12 promises, "But as many as received Him, to them He gave the right to become children of God, even those who believe in His name." If you have trusted Christ as your Savior, you are a child of the King and have every reason to hold your head high and live with the assurance of eternal glory.

Joy and peace are yours to be had. But you must make your mind up to pursue and possess them. They can be had everywhere you go and in every circumstance in which you find yourself. Allow me to close this chapter with a wonderful reminder from the pen of S.H. Payer:

What will today bring?

This is the beginning of a new day.

God has given me this day to use as I will.

I can waste it or use it for good.

What I do today is important.

Because I'm exchanging a day of my life for it.

When tomorrow comes this day will be gone forever,

Leaving in its place something I have traded for it.

I want it to be gain, not loss:

Good, not evil:

Success, not failure:

In order that I shall not regret

The price I paid for it

Because the future is just

A whole string of nows.

SHARING PIECES:

Share a time when you experienced peace in the midst of a storm.

____

____

____

____

Tell the story of someone who exemplified peace and joy during difficult circumstances.

____

____

____

____

Write out and share four directives for your life.

____

____

____

____

CONCLUSION

"WHAT YOU DO WHEN YOU DON'T HAVE TO WILL DETERMINE WHAT YOU'LL BE WHEN YOU CAN'T HELP IT." -UNKNOWN

As was mentioned before, wholeness is possible, but only if you make it so. You'll find that the enactment of each of these principles comes as a result of three main ingredients: choice, habit, and planning.

The world is in the fracturing business and will relentlessly hammer at you from all angles in any measure it can. You have to make the choice to stem the tide and reverse the effects of the world's onslaught.

Choice: This is listed first because it is the platform on which everything else rests. If you do not choose to do so, wholeness will not manifest itself in your life. Wholeness is not automatic. The world is in the *fracturing business* and will relentlessly hammer at you from all angles in any measure it can. You have to make the choice to stem the tide and reverse the effects of the world's onslaught.

Habits: When you develop habits of wholeness on a regular basis, you'll find that they become part of your being. They seem to come naturally even though it is not natural for you to have these principles as part of your personality or makeup.

An artist was asked by a man to paint a picture of an eagle. A month later, the man returned to the studio to retrieve the work of art. There before him was a beautiful rendition of a bald eagle resplendent in detail and vibrant in color. The man stood there admiring the artwork. Finally, he asked the artist, "How long did it take you to finish such a fine piece?" The artist looked at the man and replied, "thirty-five years."

Countless hours of study, miles of canvas, innumerable applications and experiments with color, and years of practice all went into creating a masterpiece that was completed in a month's time.

You must develop habits of mind and body in order to inculcate the principles that will develop into wholeness for you. It will not be easy, but it rewards you with an exciting and abundant life worth living.

Planning: Each and every day, as I settle in behind my desk, I pull out a planning sheet for the day. At the top of the page is the verse from Philippians 4:13, "I can do all things through Him who strengthens me." Below that is the lined paper on which I place all my plans for the day. Because God owns my schedule, I understand that He can interrupt it and interject whatever He wants, but I have to start with some type of plan as to how the day will be framed.

When dealing with principles, you must come up with a plan for how you can put each of them to work in your life. It's been said in many different ways, *few people plan to fail but many fail to plan and therein lies failure.* Whatever your life becomes, you must have a plan; it must be a good plan, and you have to implement the plan. Without doing each of these, you'll find that your intentions get you nowhere.

All businessmen want to be successful. All sports teams want to win. All parents want to have children on whom they can brag. But without proper planning, all people can do is hope and rely on luck. The prospects for success are not in their favor. But with a plan that is good and well executed, the chances for winning loom larger.

I watched all of this happen during a baseball game at a local university. The game was tied and the home team was up at bat in the bottom of the ninth. There were no outs when the batter dropped one into shallow right field for a double. He advanced to third on a sacrifice fly. With one out and a man on third, the coach called a time out. He summoned the batter and the runner and ordered the plan. It was a good plan, one they had practiced several times. As I sat in the stands, everything came together for the home team. As the pitcher wound up, the runner headed for home. It looked like a mistake. He would be out by a mile. But the batter made contact sending a grounder to the second baseman. He fielded the ball cleanly, but never threw the man out at first. There was no need to because by the time he caught the ball, the runner was home and the game was over.

I also saw this happen in the life of a business friend of mine. John was a planner by nature. He did his homework and worked hard at being a success. So when he told me how he grew his business, it didn't surprise me. John owned an oxygen supply company. Much of what he did was deliver oxygen tanks to hospitals, pharmacies, and homes. But when he learned of a steel mill moving into an area, he immediately bought a nearby vacant lot and put up a warehouse. Because of his proximity to the steel mill, he could quickly deliver the oxygen they needed to run the mill and his company realized a jump in profit, all because he had a plan that was good which he implemented.

Perhaps this acrostic will be helpful:

P-Plan. Evaluate your life with an honest look at each of these principles. Find an area that you feel weak in and commit to working on shoring it up.

L-Learn. Get help from those who appear to be successful in the area in which you need help. You'll discover that most of what makes you what you are is the result of what you are exposed to by way of individuals, information, and mental processing. Learn how to gather to yourself the right people, information, and the proper thinking.

When will you finally come to the place where you say "Today?" When will you stop talking about what you're going to correct, change, or do and set sail into making it happen?

A-Activate. Put your plan into practice. All the great information, intentions, and ideas will do you little good if you don't launch your plans into action.

A pastor friend of mine shared an experience with me regarding an associate pastor on his staff. He had to relieve this associate of his position because he was ineffective. It wasn't due to a lack of ability, intelligence, or ideas. It wasn't because he lacked creativity, desire, or experience. It came down to his refusal to pull the trigger on his plans. He continually brought ministry ideas to the launching stage but never pushed the "GO" button.

N-Now. Each time we travel a particular stretch of highway, my eyes catch a roadside store that specializes in beach umbrellas. These umbrellas range in all sizes and colors. I can't help but notice them no matter how hard I try. But not long ago, I also noticed a large banner they have hanging on the fence by the road. The banner reads, "You said you'd stop next time…today is next time."

When will you finally come to the place where you say "Today?" When will you stop talking about what you're going to correct, change, or do and set sail into making it happen?

In 1938 the United States was introduced to a song that continues to captivate the hearts and minds of Americans far and wide. On radios across the land Kate Smith belted out "God Bless America" and it continues to be connected to her voice. But the song almost went unheard. While stationed in the Army, Irving Berlin wrote it in 1918 but felt that it wasn't quite right for the revue he had organized. So for twenty years it lay dormant in a drawer among other pieces he had worked on. It's difficult to imagine that such a great composition could have disappeared among a clutter of ideas.

Such is the case with the principles you are now aware of. If you want your life to be different, you must do things differently. You may not get it right immediately, and it may take you a great deal of time, but one thing is certain, if you do nothing, nothing will happen. Former Czech President Vaclav Havel once said, "It is not enough to stare up the steps, we must step up the stairs."

So where does all this bring us? What is the conclusion of the matter? It is simply this: Wholeness is within your grasp! Your life can be full, abundant, and rewardingly functional. The choice is yours. The ball is in your court. The time is now!

ABOUT THE AUTHOR:

Dr. Jirgal is a 1980 graduate of Gettysburg College where he became a four-time conference champion, All-American, and inductee to the Middle Atlantic Conference *All Century Team* in the pole vault. He holds an undergraduate degree in health education and physical education. Following graduation, he taught on the high school and college level while coaching football and track in both venues. He holds masters degrees in health education, sports medicine, and divinity, as well as a doctorate in ministry.

He has been the director of Sports Medicine at Wingate University, area director for the Fellowship of Christian Athletes and has served on the staff of Hickory Grove Baptist Church in Charlotte, N. C., as well as leading Lakeview Baptist Church, in Monroe, N. C. as the Senior Pastor. He has served on the local board of directors for the Fellowship of Christian Athletes, New Orleans Baptist Seminary and the ministerial board of Wingate University. He currently serves on the board of directors for The Carolina Study Center, and Fathers in Touch ministry.

Dr. Jirgal is the founder and director of *The Jirgal Leadership Institute* where he strives to equip people for success in leadership roles. He and his wife Pam have three children, Joshua, Caleb, and Sarah. They reside in Monroe, N. C.

OTHER BOOKS BY DR. STEVE JIRGAL

The Path of a Champion

The Dirty Dozen

Dying to Live

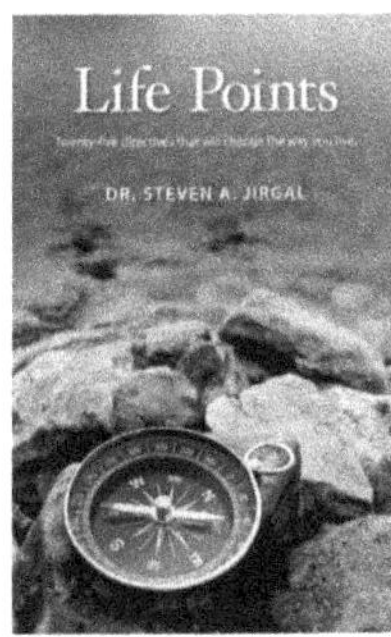

Life Points

Principles of Wholeness

Mining the Mind of King Solomon

Questions regarding any of these titles can be directed to Jirgalleadership@gmail.com

www.ingramcontent.com/pod-product-compliance
Lightning Source LLC
Chambersburg PA
CBHW020503100426
42813CB00030B/3104/J

* 9 7 8 0 9 9 6 2 6 7 5 0 2 *